Editor
Evan D. Forbes, M.S. Ed.

Editorial Project Manager
Charles Payne, M.A., M.F.A.

Editor in Chief
Sharon Coan, M.S. Ed.

Illustrator
Anna Castanato

Photo Cover Credit
Images provided by
PhotoDisc ©1994

Art Coordinator
Denice Adorno

Creative Director
Elayne Roberts

Imaging
Evan D. Forbes, M.S. Ed.

Product Manager
Phil Garcia

Publishers
Rachelle Cracchiolo, M.S. Ed.
Mary Dupuy Smith, M.S. Ed.

Bloomington
Project School

Hands-On Minds-On Science

Rain Forest

Intermediate

Author
Tricia Ball, M.S. Ed.
GATE/Mentor Teacher

Teacher Created Materials, Inc.
6421 Industry Way
Westminster, CA 92683
www.teachercreated.com
ISBN-1-57690-386-9
©2000 Teacher Created Materials, Inc.
Made in U.S.A.

Table of Contents

Introduction 4

The Scientific Method 5

Science-Process Skills 7

Organizing Your Unit 9

What Is the Rain Forest?

Just the Facts 11
Hands-On Activities

  • Locating the World's Rain Forests 13

  • Catching the Rain 14

  • Rain Forest in the Classroom 16

  • Graphing Rain Forest Plant Growth 17

  • Homemade Rain 22

What Lives in the Rain Forest?

Just the Facts 23
Hands-On Activities

  • Rain Forest in Our Classroom 24

  • Pretty as a Picture 25

  • Monocots and Dicots 26

  • Growing Ferns 28

  • Show Me the Light 30

  • Don't Get Bugged 32

  • Jaguars, Caimans and Gorillas, Oh My! 33

  • Make an African Rainstick 34

  • Creating a Motif 35

How Do Animals of the Rain Forest Live?

Just the Facts 36
Hands-On Activities

  • Butterflies and Moths 37

  • Butterflies and Moths Specimen Box 42

  • Bugs That Light the Night 45

Table of Contents *(cont.)*

What Can I Do to Save the Rain Forest?

Just the Facts 46

Hands-On Activities

   • Where Can We Begin? 47

   • Plan a Poster 50

   • Make Your Own Paper 52

Station-to-Station Activities

   • Observe 55

   • Communicate 56

   • Compare 57

   • Order 59

   • Categorize 60

   • Relate 62

   • Infer 63

   • Apply 64

Management Tools

   • Animal Information Cards 65

   • Animal Illustration Cards 76

   • Science Safety 79

   • Rain Forest Journal 80

   • My Science Activity 83

   • Investigation Planner (Option 1) 84

   • Investigation Planner (Option 2) 85

   • Rain Forest Observation Area 86

   • Assessment Forms 87

   • Super Biologist Award 90

Glossary 91

Bibliography 95

Introduction

What Is Science?

What is science to young children? Is it something that they know is a part of their world? Is it a textbook in the classroom? Is it a tadpole changing into a frog? Is it a sprouting seed, a rainy day, a boiling pot, a turning wheel, a pretty rock, or a moonlit sky? Is science fun and filled with wonder and meaning? What is science to children?

Science offers you and your eager students opportunities to explore the world around you and make connections between the things you experience. The world becomes your classroom, and you, the teacher, a guide.

Science can, and should, fill children with wonder. It should cause them to be filled with questions and the desire to discover the answers to their questions. And, once they have discovered answers, they should be actively seeking new questions to answer.

The books in this series give you and the students in your classroom the opportunity to learn from the whole of your experiences—the sights, sounds, smells, tastes, and touches, as well as what you read, write about, and do. This whole-science approach allows you to experience and understand your world as you explore science concepts and skills together.

What Is the Rain Forest?

The tropical rain forest is located near the equator. Tropical rain forests are very special places. Seven percent of the earth's land areas are tropical rain forests. They are warm all year round. The rain forest got its name because it rains every day. Some of these rains can just be showers, or they can be harsh downpours that last a few hours. These hot and humid regions have at least 75 inches (2 m) of rain a year. Temperatures in the rain forest are fairly constant. They range from 68° F (20° C) to 85° F (30° C) both day and night all year long. The days are hot and moist, and the evenings are damp and warm. It rarely gets cool in the evening in the tropical rain forest.

The Scientific Method

The "scientific method" is one of several creative and systematic processes for proving or disproving a given question following an observation. When the scientific method is used in the classroom, a basic set of guiding principles and procedures is followed in order to answer a question. However, real world science is often not as rigid as the scientific method would have us believe.

This systematic method of problem solving will be described in the paragraphs that follow.

1   Make an OBSERVATION.

The teacher presents a situation, gives a demonstration, or reads background material that interests students and prompts them to ask questions. Or students can make observations and generate questions on their own as they study a topic.

2   Select a QUESTION to investigate.

In order for students to select a question for a scientific investigation, they will have to consider the materials they have or can get, as well as the resources (books, magazines, people, etc.) actually available to them. You can help them make an inventory of their materials and resources, either individually or as a group.

Tell students that in order to successfully investigate the questions they have selected, they must be very clear about what they are asking. Discuss effective questions with your students. Depending upon their level, simplify the questions or make them more specific.

3   Make a PREDICTION (hypothesis).

Explain to students that a hypothesis is a good guess about what the answer to a question will probably be. But they do not want to make just any arbitrary guess. Encourage students to predict what they think will happen and why. In order to formulate a hypothesis, students may have to gather more information through research.

Have students practice making hypotheses with questions you give them. Tell them to pretend they have already done their research. You want them to write each hypothesis so it follows these rules:

1. It is to the point.
2. It tells what will happen, based on what the question asks.
3. It follows the subject/verb relationship of the question.

The Scientific Method *(cont.)*

4 | Develop a **PROCEDURE** to test the hypothesis.

The first thing students must do in developing a procedure (the test plan) is to determine the materials they will need.

They must state exactly what needs to be done in step-by-step order. If they do not place their directions in the right order, or if they leave out a step, it becomes difficult for someone else to follow their directions. A scientist never knows when other scientists will want to try the same experiment to see if they end up with the same results!

5 | Record the **RESULTS** of the investigation in written and picture form.

The results (data collected) of a scientific investigation are usually expressed two ways—in written form and in picture form. Both are summary statements. The written form reports the results with words. The picture form (often a chart or graph) reports the results so the information can be understood at a glance.

6 | State a **CONCLUSION** that tells what the results of the investigation mean.

The conclusion is a statement which tells the outcome of the investigation. It is drawn after the student has studied the results of the experiment, and it interprets the results in relation to the stated hypothesis. A conclusion statement may read something like either of the following: "The results show that the hypothesis is supported," or "The results show that the hypothesis is not supported." Then restate the hypothesis if it was supported or revise it if it was not supported.

7 | Record **QUESTIONS, OBSERVATIONS**, and **SUGGESTIONS** for future investigations.

Students should be encouraged to reflect on the investigations that they complete. These reflections, like those of professional scientists, may produce questions that will lead to further investigations.

Science-Process Skills

Even the youngest students blossom in their ability to make sense out of their world and succeed in scientific investigations when they learn and use the science-process skills. These are the tools that help children think and act like professional scientists.

The first five process skills on the list below are the ones that should be emphasized with young children, but all of the skills will be utilized by anyone who is involved in scientific study.

Observing

It is through the process of observation that all information is acquired. That makes this skill the most fundamental of all the process skills. Children have been making observations all their lives, but they need to be made aware of how they can use their senses and prior knowledge to gain as much information as possible from each experience. Teachers can develop this skill in children by asking questions and making statements that encourage precise observations.

Communicating

Humans have developed the ability to use language and symbols which allow them to communicate not only in the "here and now" but also over time and space as well. The accumulation of knowledge in science, as in other fields, is due to this process skill. Even young children should be able to understand the importance of researching others' communications about science and the importance of communicating their own findings in ways that are understandable and useful to others. The endangered species journal and the data-capture sheets used in this book are two ways to develop this skill.

Comparing

Once observation skills are heightened, students should begin to notice the relationships among things that they are observing. *Comparing* means noticing similarities and differences. By asking how things are alike and different or which is smaller or larger, teachers will encourage children to develop their comparison skills.

Ordering

Other relationships that students should be encouraged to observe are the linear patterns of seriation (order along a continuum: e.g., rough to smooth, large to small, bright to dim, few to many) and sequence (order along a time line or cycle). By ranking graphs, time lines, cyclical and sequence drawings and by putting many objects in order by a variety of properties, students will grow in their abilities to make precise observations about the order of nature.

Categorizing

When students group or classify objects or events according to logical rationale, they are using the process skill of categorizing. Students begin to use this skill when they group by a single property such as color. As they develop this skill, they will be attending to multiple properties in order to make categorizations; the animal classification system, for example, is one system students can categorize.

Science-Process Skills *(cont.)*

Relating

Relating, which is one of the higher-level process skills, requires student scientists to notice how objects and phenomena interact with one another and the changes caused by these interactions. An obvious example of this is the study of chemical reactions.

Inferring

Not all phenomena are directly observable because they are out of humankind's reach in terms of time, scale, and space. Some scientific knowledge must be logically inferred based on the data that is available. Much of the work of paleontologists, astronomers, and those studying the structure of matter is done by inference.

Applying

Even very young, budding scientists should begin to understand that people have used scientific knowledge in practical ways to change and improve the way we live. It is at this application level that science becomes meaningful for many students.

Applying

Inferring

Relating

Categorizing

Ordering

Comparing

Communicating

Observing

8

Organizing Your Unit

Designing a Science Lesson

In addition to the lessons presented in this unit, you will want to add lessons of your own, lessons that reflect the unique environment in which you live, as well as the interests of your students. When designing new lessons or revising old ones, try to include the following elements in your planning:

Question

Pose a question to your students that will guide them in the direction of the experiment you wish to perform. Encourage all answers, but you want to lead the students towards the experiment you are going to be doing. Remember, there must be an observation before there can be a question. (Refer to The Scientific Method, pages 5–6.)

Setting the Stage

Prepare your students for the lesson. Brainstorm to find out what students already know. Have children review books to discover what is already known about the subject. Invite them to share what they have learned.

Materials Needed for Each Group or Individual

List the materials each group or individual will need for the investigation. Include a data-capture sheet when appropriate.

Procedure

Make sure students know the steps to take to complete the activity. Whenever possible, ask them to determine the procedure. Make use of assigned roles in group work. Create (or have your students create) a data-capture sheet. Ask yourself, "How will my students record and report what they have discovered? Will they tally, measure, draw, or make a checklist? Will they make a graph? Will they need to preserve specimens?" Let students record results orally, using a videotape or audiotape recorder. For written recording, encourage students to use a variety of paper supplies such as poster board or index cards. It is also important for students to keep journals of their investigation activities. Journals can be made of lined and unlined paper. Students can design their own covers. The pages can be stapled or be put together with paper fasteners or spiral binding.

Extensions

Continue the success of the lesson. Consider which related skills or information you can tie into the lesson, like math, language arts skills, or something being learned in social studies. Make curriculum connections frequently and involve the students in making these connections. Extend the activity, whenever possible, to home investigations.

Closure

Encourage students to think about what they have learned and how the information connects to their own lives. Prepare rain forest journals using the directions on page 80. Provide an ample supply of blank and lined pages for students to use as they complete the closure activities. Allow time for students to record their thoughts and pictures in their journals.

Organizing Your Unit *(cont.)*

Structuring Student Groups for Scientific Investigations

Using cooperative learning strategies in conjunction with hands-on and discovery learning methods will benefit all the students taking part in the investigation.

Cooperative Learning Strategies

1. In cooperative learning, all group members need to work together to accomplish the task.
2. Cooperative learning groups should be heterogeneous.
3. Cooperative learning activities need to be designed so that each student contributes to the group and individual group members can be assessed on their performance.
4. Cooperative learning teams need to know the social as well as the academic objectives of a lesson.

Cooperative Learning Groups

Groups can be determined many ways for the scientific investigations in your class. Here is one way of forming groups that has proven to be successful in intermediate classrooms.

*   **The Team Leader**—scientist in charge of reading directions and setting up equipment.
*   **The Biologist**—scientist in charge of carrying out directions (can be more than one student).
*   **The Stenographer**—scientist in charge of recording all of the information.
*   **The Transcriber**—scientist who translates notes and communicates findings.

If the groups remain the same for more than one investigation, require each group to vary the people chosen for each job. All group members should get a chance to try each job at least once.

Using Centers for Scientific Investigations

Set up stations for each investigation. To accommodate several groups at a time, stations may be duplicated for the same investigation. Each station should contain directions for the activity, all necessary materials (or a list of materials for investigators to gather), a list of words (a word bank) which students may need for writing and speaking about the experience, and any data-capture sheets or needed materials for recording and reporting data and findings.

Station-to-Station Activities are on pages 55–64. Model and demonstrate each of the activities for the whole group. Have directions at each station. During the modeling session, have a student read the directions aloud while the teacher carries out the activity. When all students understand what they must do, let small groups conduct the investigations at the centers. You may wish to have a few groups working at the centers while others are occupied with other activities. In this case, you will want to set up a rotation schedule so all groups have a chance to work at the centers.

Assign each team to a station, and after they complete the task described, help them rotate in a clockwise order to the other stations. If some groups finish earlier than others, be prepared with another unit-related activity to keep students focused on main concepts. After all rotations have been made by all groups, come together as a class to discuss what was learned.

Just the Facts

Are Rain Forests the Same as Jungles?

Although most people will quickly answer "yes" to that question, the two are not actually the same. Rain forests naturally occur in a band around Earth between the Tropic of Capricorn (23º S latitude) and the Tropic of Cancer (23º N latitude). The majority of the rain forests are found in Central America and the northern half of South America, in India, Southeast Asia, Australia and in 2/3 of central Africa. There are also rain forests in the East Indies, the Philippines, the West Indies, and even in parts of Washington state and Florida.

Rain forests are sometimes called jungles because of the thick and abundant vegetation found there. Jungles are often described as an area of thick, tangled plant growth at ground level. People think of the jungle as a place where literary characters such as Tarzan and Mowgli live and monkeys swing from the vines of enormous trees, but not all rain forests are jungles.

Rain forests are sometimes categorized according to their latitudes, altitudes, and environmental conditions. Generally, rain forests are classified as either equatorial or subtropical. There are four major types of rain forests: equatorial, subtropical, monsoon and montane or high altitude. Each forest has a distinct set of characteristics to distinguish it from the other.

The Equatorial Rain Forest

The equatorial rain forests are located in South America, Africa, and the Malaysian region. These areas contain the densest jungles in the world. The largest unbroken tract of forest is found in Brazil in the area surrounding the Amazon River. Africa also contains the largest jungle area surrounding the Congo River. The Amazon rain forest is home to more than 40–50% of all the living plant and animal species known to man. Scientists speculate that there are over 50,000 species of plants that have never been studied or named in the Amazon Basin. Fifty years ago the Amazon rain forest covered one-half the continent of Africa and was virtually unexplored. Today scientists are concerned about its exploitation and its extinction. The equatorial rain forest is a hot, humid region covering about 7% of Earth's surface. Rainfall in the jungle is more than 60 inches (150 centimeters) a year and may be as high as 400 inches (1,000 centimeters). The average temperature is 68–90º F. The relative humidity in the equatorial rain forest is normally from 75 to 100 percent. Rainfall nearest the equator is continual throughout the year.

The Subtropical Rain Forest

The subtropical rain forest differs from the equatorial one inasmuch as it has more seasonal changes. The temperature in this area may vary slightly over the year, but the rainfall is distributed unevenly. Located in Central America, the West Indies, India, Madagascar, Southeast Asia, and the Philippines, these regions have noticeably wet and dry seasons. The temperature in these regions may vary slightly between 68 degrees F. (20º C) to above 90 degrees F (32º C). The Everglades in southern Florida is the only area in the United States that can be classified as jungle.

Just the Facts *(cont.)*

The Monsoon Forest

Monsoon forests receive high amounts of rainfall distributed evenly throughout the year. Monsoons are climatic situations of heavy and continual rainfall during spring and summer, followed by a distinct dry season in the fall and winter. Vegetation in the monsoon rain forest is not as dense as that of the tropical rain forest canopy, but it has more foliage in the lower levels. Monsoon rain forests are located in Southeast Asia, Java, and northeastern Australia. There are monsoon jungles in West Africa and South America.

The Montane Forest

The montane rain forest or high altitude jungles do not meet the warm-unvarying temperature standards that are characteristic of a typical rain forest. In the montane forest temperatures are wide-ranging due to their high elevation. Located in altitudes that range from 3,000 feet (900 meters) to more than 5,000 feet (1,500 meters) are the dense, constantly wet regions that qualify as jungles. Montanes are located throughout the tropics with the most notable in Central Africa and New Guinea.

Other warm, perpetually humid climatic conditions are sometimes considered rain forests. These are the broadleaf-tree forests of the coastal areas of North and South Carolina and Georgia in the southeastern part of the United States. These areas have dense underbrush and a canopy of medium-sized trees. The annual rainfall is high and the seasonal temperature warm, although nowhere near that of the tropical rain forest. In addition, the mangrove forests found along many coastlines in the world are called rain forests because of the closeness their trees and their roots give the appearance of the jungle habitat.

12

Locating the World's Rain Forests

Directions: On the map below locate the major rain forests. Color the equatorial rain forests **green**. Color the subtropical rain forests **yellow**. Color the monsoon rain forests **blue**. Color the montane rain forests **red**.

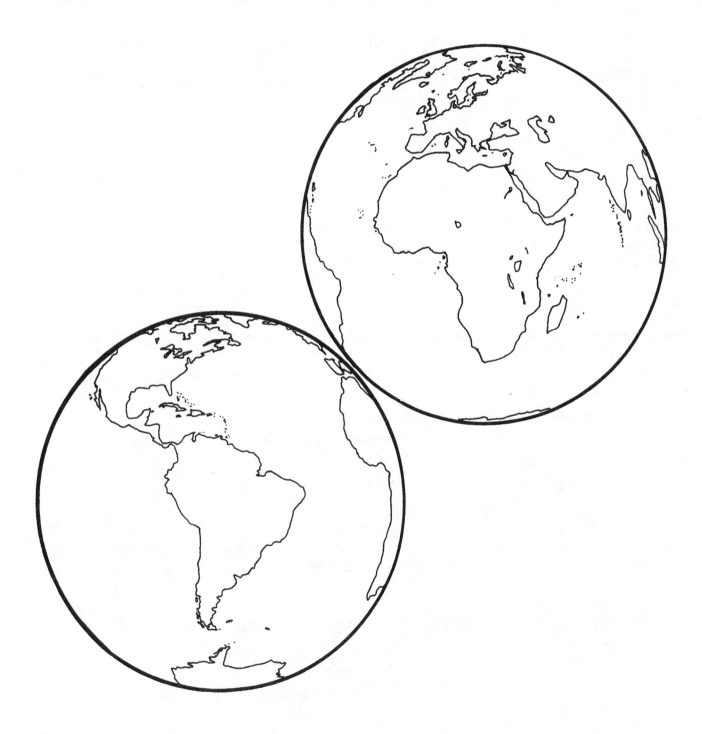

Catching the Rain

Question

How can we measure rainfall?

Setting the Stage

- Begin a dialog with your class by asking the students how much rain they think falls daily in the rain forest.
- Discuss the rainfall in your area and compare that to the rainfall the students predicted for the rain forest.
- Remind students that when it rains heavily outside, they often complain and grumble. Can they imagine what it would be like to live in the rain forest?

Materials Needed for Each Group

- straight-sided water glass or pan
- ruler or a meter stick
- paper
- pencil
- rain
- Recording the Rain chart (page 15)

Procedure

1. When rain is expected, take the pan or glass outside to a place where there are no buildings, walls, trees, or obstructions.
2. As soon as possible after the rain stops, use the ruler to measure the amount of water in the container.
3. Rainfall is usually reported in inches or centimeters.
4. Keep a chart of the rainfall in your area for a week or a month.
5. Record your results on the Recording the Rain chart.
6. Compare the results to the facts you have learned about rain in the rain forest.

Extension

Investigate how rain is formed. Prepare a report for your classmates. Each student might desire to be a meterologist for a day and report the daily weather.

Closure

Write a paragraph on what it might be like to be an insect in the rain forest.

Catching the Rain *(cont.)*

Recording the Rain

	Monday	Tuesday	Wednesday	Thursday	Friday
Week 1					
Week 2					
Week 3					
Week 4					

Number of Inches/Centimeters of Rain

Write your comparison of the amount of rainfall in your area over one month as compared to the amount in the rain forest.

_____

_____

_____

_____

_____

_____

_____

Rain Forest in the Classroom

Question

Is it possible to create a rain forest in the classroom?

Setting the Stage

- Elicit from the students all the elements that plants and trees need to thrive and live in the rain forest.
- Review with students the structure of the rain forest, and suggest each rain forest is different and may not contain all of the same plants.
- Make a list of all the conditions that make the tropics excellent for the lush foliage of the plants in the rain forest.

Materials Needed for the Class

- 15-gallon aquarium with a full glass top or a sheet of acrylic plastic
- sand and gravel—enough to cover the bottom of the aquarium about 2" (5 cm) deep
- charcoal
- potting soil
- water
- various houseplants—can be obtained at your local nursery (e.g., dieffenbachia, schefflera, dracaena, philodendron, fern, liverwort, moss, prayer plant, bromeliads

Procedure

1. Place about 2" (5 cm) of sand and gravel mixture on the bottom of the tank.
2. Place about 1" (2.5 cm) of charcoal on top of the gravel/sand mixture.
3. Complete the floor by layering about 3"–4" (7.5–8 cm) of potting soil on top of the charcoal.
4. Moisten the soil with water, and then plant the plants carefully.
5. Water plants with about two cups (500 mL) of water.
6. Cover with glass or acrylic sheet, leaving a small space for air.
7. Place the terrarium in a location where it will receive morning sunlight.

Note: Water should recycle naturally through the aquarium. Condensation will develop as a result of evaporation and transpiration, forming water droplets which will rain down on the micro rain forest. If the system seems too dry, add a little water. If it seems too wet, raise the acrylic plastic a bit.

Extension

After about 10 days, you can introduce invertebrates, reptiles, and amphibians slowly into the terrarium. Place one or two a day and be careful not to overload the environment with too many things. Some examples suitable for your rain forest terrarium include the following: crickets, tree frogs, cockroaches, salamanders, centipeds, newts, millipeds, anoles, snails, and slugs.

Closure

Write an entry in your journal each day to record the happenings of the animal life in your rain forest.

Graphing Rain Forest Plant Growth

Question

Do the plants in the rain forest grow at a steady rate?

Setting the Stage

- Elicit from your class the facts they know about the behavior of plants. Have them write these facts in their rain forest journals.
- Have the class make predictions about the growth of the plants in the rain forest. Do they think the plants will grow faster than average? What factors in the rain forest might affect plant growth?

Materials Needed for Each Individual

- student rain forest journal
- graphing the rain forest work sheets (pages 18–21)

Procedure

1. Using the information students recorded in their rain forest journals, have them plot the growth of the plants over the four-week period on the graphs on the next four pages.
2. Have students use different colors for each week. This will enable them to visualize the different rates of plant growth.

Extension

The same procedure can be used if animal life has been introduced into the rain forest environment. Simply change the wording from plants to animals.

Closure

Have students predict what will happen in the rain forest if man cuts down a few trees/plants. Record the predictions on a chart and see what happens over time.

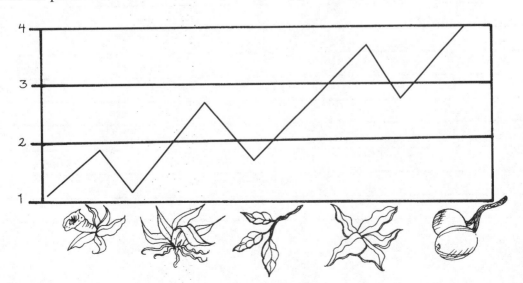

Graphing Rain Forest Plant Growth *(cont.)*

Rain Forest Growth

Week 1—Planting

Write a brief description of how your rain forest looks. Draw a picture of your rain forest. Measure the height of each plant and record the information below.

_____

_____

_____

_____

Plant Sizes

Name of Plant	Height
1.	
2.	
3.	
4.	
5.	
6.	
7.	
8.	
9.	
10.	

Graphing Rain Forest Plant Growth *(cont.)*

Rain Forest Growth *(cont.)*

Week 2

Write a brief description of how your rain forest looks. Draw a picture of your rain forest. Measure the height of each plant and record the information below.

_____

_____

_____

_____

Plant Sizes

Name of Plant	Height
1.	
2.	
3.	
4.	
5.	
6.	
7.	
8.	
9.	
10.	

Graphing Rain Forest Plant Growth *(cont.)*

Rain Forest Growth *(cont.)*

Week 3

Write a brief description of how your rain forest looks. Draw a picture of your rain forest. Measure the height of each plant and record the information below.

_____

_____

_____

_____

Plant Sizes

	Name of Plant	Height
1.		
2.		
3.		
4.		
5.		
6.		
7.		
8.		
9.		
10.		

Graphing Rain Forest Plant Growth *(cont.)*

Rain Forest Growth *(cont.)*

Week 4

Write a brief description of how your rain forest looks. Draw a picture of your rain forest. Measure the height of each plant and record the information below.

_____

_____

_____

_____

Plant Sizes

Name of Plant	Height
1.	
2.	
3.	
4.	
5.	
6.	
7.	
8.	
9.	
10.	

Homemade Rain

Question

Where does all the rain in the rain forest come from?

Setting the Stage

- "It's raining, it's pouring . . ." goes the old song. But where does the rain come from?
- Discuss the atmospheric conditions needed for it to rain.
- Show super-saturation by soaking a sponge. Then amaze the class with the following demonstration.

Materials Needed for the Teacher

- a large metal spoon or soup ladle
- a kettle one-quarter filled with water
- hot plate

Procedure

1. Put the spoon or ladle into the freezer to cool it. A bowl of ice will work too.
2. When the spoon is ice cold, turn on the kettle. As the water in the kettle heats up, it turns into steam. Most people think the white vapor coming from the kettle is steam, but it is not. Real steam is invisible. If you look closely, but not too closely, you'll see a space between the kettle and where the white vapor starts. That space is steam. As steam meets the air outside the kettle, it cools and becomes water vapor which is visible as a white cloud.
3. When the water is boiling, hold the cold spoon in the white vapor coming form the kettle's pour spout.
4. In a few seconds, it will be raining.

Extensions

- Record the weather for a week or two. Discuss the relationship between the temperature, air mass, and the humidity in the air.
- Establish the requirements needed for rain and how they relate to the conditions in the rain forest.

Closure

In your rain forest journal, write the following journal entry. What is rain, and what atmospheric conditions are present in the rain forest that cause it to rain daily?

22

Just the Facts

The rain forest is really four different worlds in one. These worlds are stacked one on top of each other like building blocks.

The Emergent Layer

The emergent layer is the uppermost layer of the rain forest. It is formed of the isolated tops of the tallest trees, which rise as much as 300 feet (91 m) above the forest floor. The emergent layer is home to the great birds of prey which use the tops of trees for nesting as well as for sighting prey. In parts of Asia and the East Indies, trees occasionally reach heights of 200 feet (61 m).

The Canopy

Below the giant trees are ones whose tops converge horizontally to form a dense upper canopy, generally 150 to 250 feet (46 to 76 m) above the ground. The canopy is composed of the crowns of closely spaced trees. The canopy is sunny and offers the most food and shelter in the rain forest. The canopy supports the majority of animal life.

The Understory

Below the upper canopy there is often an open space referred to as a second canopy or understory. It is created by smaller trees and other vegetation. These trees wait for a chance to reach the sun. If a mature tree falls, sunlight reaches these stunted trees, allowing them to reach their mature height. If not, they live their lives as immature saplings.

The Shrub Layer

The shrub layer is not a dense one as the upper two layers are. Plants are widely scattered. In this layer you will find ground-dwelling mammals taking their food.

The Floor or Ground Layer

The floor or ground layer is made up of low-growing plants. The floor of the rain forest is penetrated by less than one percent of the sunlight from above. There you can find the floor lightly covered by ground vegetation with extensive spacing between between the vines and tree trunks. This area of the rain forest can be traversed relatively easily. The relative humidity and the temperature on the floor of the rain forest are more constant than anywhere else in the forest.

Rain Forest in Our Classroom

Question

What does a rain forest look like?

Setting the Stage

- It is often difficult for students to realize the size of a rain forest from books or activities. Here is an activity that gives some idea about size proportion to your students.
- Discuss with your class the concept of size. How big do they think the trees in the rain forest are? as big as a building? a maple or oak tree? What things might be in a rain forest?

Materials Needed for the Class

- assorted books on the rain forest—see Bibliography
- construction paper—assorted colors
- scissors, glue, crayons, markers
- long sheets of brown butcher paper—enough to construct a floor-to-ceiling tree
- green butcher paper to construct palm-like leaves

Procedure

1. Have students research plants and animals that live in the rain forest.
2. With the students working in teams, have the teams draw, color, and cut out a variety of plants and animals that are found in the rain forest.
3. While the students are constructing the wildlife, twist long sheets of brown butcher paper into the trunk and branches of a tree. Ambitious teachers can construct more than one to give the feeling of the understory and canopy.
4. Mount the trunk and branches of the tree to the ceiling and walls in a corner of the room. Have the branches extend over the students' desks to reconstruct the feeling of the rain forest.
5. Cut giant palm fronds, banana leaves, or leaves of other rain forest trees and attach them to the branches. Make sure they hang down over your students.
6. After the students have completed their animals and plants, arrange them in the layers of the rain forest in which you would find them.
7. If floor space allows, spread some burlap or blankets on the floor to represent the ground in the rain forest.

Extension

This rain forest makes a wonderful reading corner for the students. It can be left up all year.

Closure

In your rain forest journal, write for young children three to six years old a story about an adventure in the rain forest.

Pretty as a Picture

Question

How can we learn about different types of plants and their beauty?

Setting the Stage

- Discuss the diversity of plant life found in the rain forest.
- The amount of plant life in the jungle is unrivaled by any other habitat in the world. Millions of years of uniform, wet climate have made the rain forest home to more than 50,000 species of plants alone. Discuss the symmetry found in flowers and foliage of the plants in your area. Many of them have similarities to those in the rain forest.

Materials Needed for Each Individual

- two pieces of 18" x 12" (45 cm x 30 cm) construction paper
- scissors
- crayons
- waxed paper
- glue
- an iron

Procedure

1. Have students collect the local plant life that they think most resembles plants found in the rain forest. Ferns and moss spores are some suggestions.
2. Arrange the specimens on a sheet of construction paper. Using scissors, shave some different-colored crayons around the plant life. Shavings should be small.
3. Place a sheet of waxed paper equal in size to the construction paper over the plant specimens and shavings.
4. With the iron set to the lowest heat, press the picture, moving slowly from one side to another. This should weld the picture together.
5. Make a border for your picture from the second sheet of construction paper.
6. Glue the border down securely.

Extension

This project can be used in a variety of ways for many projects—a cover for a book of poems about the rain forest or a place mat for a rain forest food tasting.

Closure

Many products come from the rain forest. Research some of the ones you may use in your home and write about them in your journal. Some suggestions are: rubber, coffee, raffia, resin, wood, fibers, etc.

Monocots and Dicots

Question

Can you distinguish between monocots and dicots?

Setting the Stage

- Have students define the term *angiosperm*.
- Write the words *monocot* and *dicot* on the board. Ask students if they know what the two words mean. Some students may have already been familiar with the terms from other classes or from their own research. If this is so, allow them to explain to the others the differences between these two types of angiosperms. If not, allow for speculation.

Materials Needed for Each Group

- a variety of leaves, roots, stems, and flowers from flowering plants
- magnifying glasses
- craft knife
- copy of Monocot and Dicot Fact Sheet (page 27), one per student

    Note to the teacher: You may want extra supervision when students use the craft knives.

Procedure *(Student Instructions)*

1. Compare your leaves, roots, stems, and flowers to the ones found on your Monocot and Dicot Fact Sheet (page 27).
2. Divide up the monocots and dicots, noting similarities and differences.
3. Record the information on a separate piece of paper.

Extensions

- Have students list edible monocots and dicots and nonedible monocots and dicots.
- Have students trace shapes of flowers and leaves. Have them compare their traced shapes to geometric shapes they learned in math. Have them organize their shapes according to their geometric patterns.
- Have students plant seeds from monocots and dicots to see if there are any differences in germination.
- Have students use the seeds they have gathered to make a mosaic of a flower and its parts.

Closure

Have students draw and label in their plant journals the parts of a monocot and a dicot seed. Have them explain the similarities and differences between the two.

Monocots and Dicots *(cont.)*

Monocot and Dicot Fact Sheet

Characteristic Features:

Cotyledon	Leaf
Root	Dicot Sepal
Stem	Monocot Sepal
Xylem	Petal
Cambium	Stamen
Phloem	Pistil

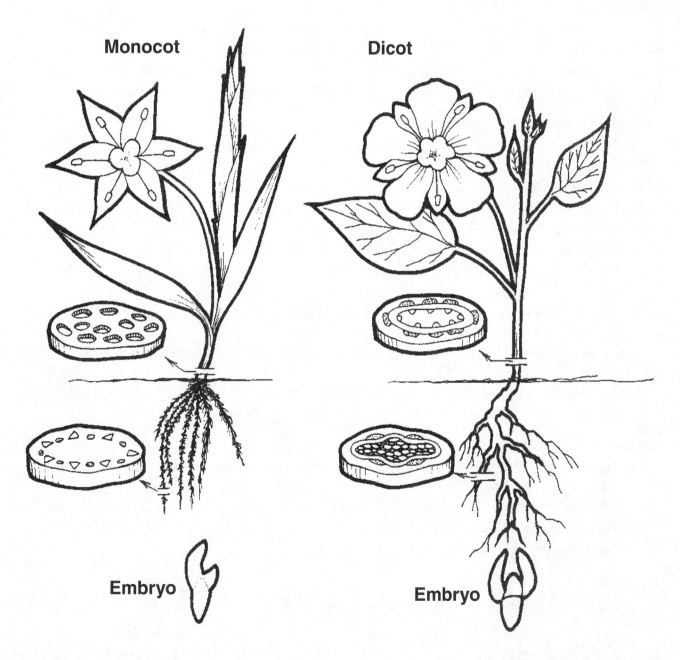

Growing Ferns

Question

Is it possible to grow ferns indoors?

Setting the Stage

- Ask students what types of plants grow in their homes. By now many of them should be well aware of the different types of plants.
- Ask students if they have any ferns growing in their gardens. With parent permission, perhaps they could bring in some cuttings for the class to examine.
- Discuss with students the needs of a plant: soil, water, air, and sunlight. Have students try to determine the best way to grow plants in the classroom.

Materials Needed for Entire Class

- five-gallon (20 L) water jar
- several tiny plants (e.g., ferns, mosses, etc.)
- newspaper
- bag of potting soil
- yard or meter stick
- data-capture sheet (page 29), one per student

Note to the teacher: You may choose to have students prepare more than one terrarium.

Procedure *(Student Instructions)*

1. Spread newspaper over your desk and floor to catch any soil that may fall.
2. Fill 1/2 of the jar with potting soil.
3. Water the soil until it is evenly wet but the water has not puddled.
4. Carefully decide where you want your plants located. Once they are placed in the jar, you will not be able to easily move them.
5. Dig a hole with your long stick. (A pointer works very well.)
6. Gently push the plant into the neck of the jar and use the stick to position it over the hole.
7. Pack the soil around the roots of the plant with the stick until it is securely fastened.
8. Repeat the same procedure for the rest of your plants. Care must be taken not to overplant. The plants will grow to full size inside the jar.
9. Water the jar sparingly. Moisture from the soil and the plants will form on the sides of the bottle and trickle down to the soil.
10. Place the jar in the sunlight or partial shade and watch the plants grow.
11. After one week draw a picture of what your terrarium looks like.

Extensions

- Have students grow spore-bearing plants in a flower pot with some soil. Have them place a frond on top of the soil. Keep the pot watered and in a shady place and watch your plant grow.
- Have students research other ways of growing gardens indoors.
- Have a class discussion about hydroponics.
- Have students make a collage of fern fronds.

Closure

Have students keep in their plant journals a weekly log of how their garden grows.

Growing Ferns *(cont.)*

Draw a picture of your terrarium.

Show Me the Light

Question

What will a tree or a plant do when it is deprived of sunlight?

Setting the Stage

One feature of the natural, undisturbed rain forest is the layering effect created by the different heights of trees and other vegetation. Discuss the various layers of the jungle with the students. Explain how the dense foliage of the plants and trees blocks the sunlight from the floor of the rain forest. Elict from the students how they think the absence of light might affect plant growth.

Materials Needed for the Class

- a syngonium "arrow leaf" plant from a local nursery
- scissors or knife
- cardboard box—tall enough to cover the plant without bending the leaves
- copy of Helio Log (page 31), one per student
- pen or pencil

Procedure

1. Cut a 3" (7.5 cm) square "window" in one side of the box.
2. Now find a sunny spot in the classroom where your plant can grow undisturbed for several days. Carefully observe the position your plant's leaves are facing. They should be facing in all directions. Note your observations on the Helio Log. Helio in Greek means "sun."
3. Now place the box over the plant. Note on the log the date and time you covered the plant as well as the direction the window is facing. Keep the plant covered at all times, except for a few moments when the syngonium may need watering.
4. After approximately 48 hours, uncover the plant. Notice anything different about the plant? Record your observations on your Helio Log.

Extension

This demonstration can be done with different species of plants to see if they will react to light deprivation in the same manner. It is also fun to purchase two plants of identical size and to compare and contrast the results of each after the light-deprived plant is removed from the box and what happens to it if it is then allowed to get sunlight.

Closure

In your rain forest journal, write about the following: Why is it that the foliage of most trees in the rain forest is not at the base or even in the middle of the tree but at the very tiptop?

Show Me the Light *(cont.)*

Helio Log

Plant Specifications:

Measure the plant from its base to the top of its tallest leaf.

Our Plant's Height _____

Measure the width across the widest part of your plant.

Our Plant's Width _____

Day One Observations:

_____

_____

_____

_____

Day Two Observations:

_____

_____

_____

_____

Draw a picture of your plant.

Day One	**Day Two**

Don't Get Bugged!

Question

What effect do ants and worms have on the rain forest?

Setting the Stage

- Although many students are familiar with the more popular animals of the rain forest, there is abundant life that lives on or in the forest floor. Discuss the types of animals or insects that live in the rain forest.

- Have students each draw a tree in their journals. Divide the tree into four sections. Label the sections to correspond to the layers in the jungle. As you discuss the animal life, have the students write the animal's name in the correct layer in which it lives.

Materials Needed for the Class

- large quart size glass jar with a lid
- soil
- ants or one or two earthworms dug from the ground
- small pieces of leaves or food crumbs for nourishment

Procedure

1. Fill the jar with soil.
2. Carefully put the worms or ants in the jar.
3. Sprinkle food on the soil and cover the jar securely with the lid.
4. Place it in a cool spot in the classroom and watch.

Extension

Ants and earthworms are fascinating creatures to watch. Ants are tireless, and many students will be curious about the fortitude and determination the ants have. Earthworms are super tunnelers, and the students will observe soil aeration firsthand. If funds are available, an ant farm is a wonderful addition to any classroom. They can be purchased from a science supply house and will provide hours of learning for your class.

Closure

Research the adaptations an ant and an earthworm might make to survive in the rain forest.

32

Jaguars, Caimans and Gorillas, Oh My!

Question

How do animals protect themselves from other animals in the jungle?

Setting the Stage

- The African rain forest is the home of some of the largest and most varied wildlife populations in the world. However, not all the animals of the rain forest are land animals. Some animals live in and on the tall branches of the trees. These animals are some of the most colorful inhabitants of the rain forest. There are the butterflies and parrots and other exotic birds that call the rain forest home. Have the students research the butterflies and birds that live in the rain forest.
- Discuss how these animals and birds have adapted themselves to their habitats.

Materials Needed for the Class

- assorted magazines (For Example, *National Geographic*, *Nature*, and *Zoo News*, a publication of the San Diego Zoo in California, have wonderful color pictures in them.)
- large sheets of assorted colored construction paper
- glue
- scissors

Procedure

1. Choose one type of animal, bird, reptile, or amphibian that lives in the rain forest.
2. Search through the magazines for that animal in various scenes that depict their lives in the jungle.
3. Carefully cut the pictures out of the magazines.
4. Glue them to your construction paper.
5. Title your picture or collage.

Extension

Some animal pictures lend themselves to captions. Have the students choose one or two pictures and write captions for them. Discuss what a caption is and have some examples for them to see. Cartoons and the comics in the newspaper are a good source for these. There are also animal pictures and cute captions on calendars that might be in your classroom.

Closure

In your rain forest journal, write a story about what your animal might be thinking in the pictures you created. You might want to write about a day in the life of your creature. Be imaginative.

Make an African Rainstick

Question

What does the rain in the rain forest sound like?

Setting the Stage

Ask the students what they think the rain in the rain forest sounds like. Do they think it is the same sound as the rain we hear on the roof? Is it the driving rain we might hear during a storm? The rain in the jungle is often a soft-sounding rain. The tribes in Africa and South America both use a musical instrument to recreate the sound of the rain. The rainstick is an ancient percussion instrument that is made from a petrified cactus plant or from a hollow tree trunk. It is filled with various sizes of seeds, pebbles, and shells for sound.

Materials Needed for Each Individual

- large cardboard tube, 4 feet (1 m) or longer and approximately 1/4–1/2-inch (.625–1.25 cm) thick (If these are not available, tubing from wrapping paper will work.)
- various-size nails
- cardboard
- hammer
- scissors
- masking tape
- rice, seeds, beans
- tiny shells or pebbles

Procedure

1. Hammer long and short nails into the cardboard tube in a spiral.
2. Cut two cardboard circles, two inches (5 cm) bigger on all sides than the circumference of the tube, and then cut slits.
3. Cover one end of the tube with a circle, fold down the slits, and tape down the ends.
4. Fill one-tenth of the tube with the seeds, rice, beans, and tiny shells.
5. Seal the other end of the tube with the remaining circle, following steps two and three.
6. Then have the students make an African motif strip to decorate the rainstick. (See creating a Motif, page 35.)

Extension

Create other African instruments and play your own music. Learn about other ways the African and South American tribes created the sounds found in nature.

Closure

Complete your rainstick by creating a motif.

34

Creating a Motif

Question

What types of designs did the African and South American tribes decorate their rainsticks?

Setting the Stage

Discuss with the class the various types of materials found in the rain forest that the tribes could use to decorate their sticks—dried leaves, bark to make carvings, vines and roots to paint with. In Africa, a simple stamp print carved from the bark of the calabash tree was used for decoration. The black dye from the badie tree was used to print. Some of the imprints had symbolic meaning. Some were just used for decoration.

Materials Needed for Each Individual

- art tape or strips of different-colored construction paper
- small potatoes
- butter knife or plastic knife
- black tempera paint

Procedure

1. Cut the potato in half.
2. Using the knife, cut away shapes and wedges.
3. Dip the potato into the black tempera paint, and then stamp repeatedly onto the art tape or paper strip.
4. Have the students trade stamps with each other for their next strip.
5. When they are dry carefully wrap the art strips around the tube or glue the construction paper around the tube.
6. Allow the strips to dry overnight. Then the tube can be turned slowly from side to side to recreate the rain sound.

Closure

Now that your rainstick has a design and has dried, try it out.

Just the Facts

Even though the rain forest is so small, it is home to more than half the world's plant and animal life. There are more plants and animals in the tropical rain forest than in all of Europe! Animal life is quite different here than in the taiga, tundra, or the other forests. In the tropical rain forest, you can see trees as tall as 17-story buildings, watch brilliantly colored birds flying in the thick vegetation, and hear the chatter of monkeys. There are over 1,500 species of butterflies in the rain forest. Butterflies do not start out being butterflies. Before there is a butterfly, there is a fluffy, creepy, crawling insect called a caterpillar. In fact, a butterfly goes through a series of life stages called *metamorphosis.* Learn about metamorphosis in the quick-change activity that follows. Like the animals of the other biomes, the animals in the tropical rain forest are also suited to their environment. Some monkeys and lemurs use their tails to swing through trees in search of food. Colorful birds such as parrots, toucans, and budgies or parakeets are protected by their brilliant colors. They blend into the brightly colored flowers that fill the rain forest all year long. Rather than hide themselves in the thick underbrush of the rain forest floor, many animals use their bright coloring as a warning to other animals to stay away.

Frogs in the rain forest come in many colors. Many are quite beautiful to look at, but their skins are poisonous. Hunters rub their arrows on the backs of frogs to create lethal weapons.

Other creatures found in the rain forest are the American click beetles. They measure only 1.5" (3.75 cm) in length, but you can hear their clicking sounds throughout the world's rain forests. Click beetles are unusual in another way. They are a kind of firefly and have glowing abdomens. Learn just how these insects glow by completing "Bugs That Light the Night" (page 45).

In the rain forest there are animals that use their claws for grasping the trees, animals that use their tails for grabbing vines, animals with toes that stick to trees, and animals that fly and leap. Birds and butterflies are not the only animals in the rain forest that fly. In the rain forests of North America, Asia, and Africa, there are flying squirrels and lizards. These animals have extra flaps of skin that enable them to catch the air and float on the air currents. The flying squirrels have skin flaps that extend from their front legs to their hind legs. The skin stretches out like a kite when they leap. The insect-eating lizards also have along the sides of their bodies an extra flap of skin that helps them glide through the air. It is important to remember that these animals are not flyers like the birds. They only use air currents and glide.

Butterflies and Moths

Question

Can we identify the butterflies or moths that live in our biome?

Setting the Stage

- Tell students the rain forest is alive with beautiful insects. They come in all colors and shapes. They might see a variety of these "lepidoptera" in their own backyards. Ask them if they know what these creatures are. They are the butterfly and the moth.

- Explain to students that the tropics are located near the equator and that it is difficult to travel there to experience the beautiful butterflies and moths firsthand. In this activity we will become familiar with some common butterflies and moths and keep caterpillars in captivity. The above scenario will pique students' interest for the "Butterflies and Moths" activity.

Materials Needed for Each Individual

- a copy of "Butterfly and Moth Identification" (pages 38–41)
- scissors
- tagboard or cardboard for mounting
- colored markers or crayons
- books on butterflies and moths
- paper fasteners
- one sheet of construction paper

Procedure

1. Make copies of "Butterfly and Moth Identification" for each student.
2. Have students cut out the pictures of the butterflies and moths and mount them on the cardboard.
3. Have students locate the butterflies and the moths in a book or encyclopedia and color them the correct colors.
4. Have students make a facts list on the back of the card.
5. Have students cut a piece of construction paper to fit their cards and design a cover for their collection.
6. Have students fasten their cards and cover together to make a booklet.

Extensions

- Have students use the drawings of butterflies and moths on pages 38 and 40 to identify the ones that live in their biome.
- Have students identify the differences between a moth and a butterfly. Can you tell just by looking? What other facts do you need to know?

Closures

- In their animal journals, have students record and respond to the following questions: What impact does the butterfly have on our environment? What would be different if there were no butterflies?
- Have them read some books on butterflies and moths.

Butterflies and Moths *(cont.)*

Butterfly Identification

Common Sulphur Butterfly

Monarch Butterfly

Buckeye Butterfly

Cabbage White Butterfly

Painted Lady Butterfly

Tiger Swallowtail Butterfly

Butterflies and Moths *(cont.)*

Butterfly Identification *(cont.)*

Monarch Butterfly

Wingspan: 3.5 to 4" (8.75 to 10 cm)

Range: Includes the entire United States

This butterfly is active during the day. In the fall it travels south or migrates for the winter. In the spring, the monarch mates and then begins its return trip northward.

Common Sulphur Butterfly

Wingspan: 1.5 to 2" (3.75 to 5 cm)

Range: Includes all of United States except for many parts of Florida

This butterfly is active during the day. The common sulphur can be found in most open spaces. It likes farmland because of its eating habits.

Cabbage White Butterfly

Wingspan: 1.25 to 2" (3 to 5 cm)

Range: Includes the entire United States and Hawaii

This butterfly is active during the day. It likes fields and gardens.

Buckeye Butterfly

Wingspan: 2 to 2.33" (5 to 6 cm)

Range: Includes the entire United States

This butterfly is an adult during the winter months.

Painted Lady Butterfly

Wingspan: 1.75 to 2.5" (4 to 6.25 cm)

Range: Includes the entire United States

This butterfly is active during the day. It likes open places. The painted lady also migrates or travels south for the winter.

Tiger Swallowtail Butterfly

Wingspan: 3.25 to 5.5" (8 to 13.75 cm)

Range: Includes central and eastern United States

This butterfly is active during the day. It lives in many places, including woodland clearings, parks, and gardens. It can also be found by roadsides and rivers.

Butterflies and Moths (cont.)

Moth Identification

Luna Moth

Gypsy Moth

Achemon Sphinx Moth

Twin-spotted Sphinx Moth

Acrea Moth

Polyphemus Moth

Butterflies and Moths *(cont.)*

Moth Identification *(cont.)*

Luna Moth
Wingspan: 3.25 to 5" (8 to 12.5 cm)

Range: Includes eastern United States

This moth is active at night. Because of its size, shape, and color, it is one of the most spectacular of all moths.

Gypsy Moth
Wingspan: male—1.25 to 1.5" (2 to 3.75 cm), female—2.25 to 2.75" (5.5 to 7 cm)

Range: Includes eastern United States

This moth is active at night. It is mostly known as a pest of fruit and deciduous trees. It lives for only a few days or weeks.

Achemon Sphinx Moth
Wingspan: 3 to 4" (7.5 to 10 cm)

Range: Includes the entire United States

Adult sphinx moths are powerful flyers. They feed on nectar.

Twin-spotted Sphinx Moth
Wingspan: 2 to 3.25" (5 to 8 cm)

Range: Includes all of the United States

This moth is active at night. It lives on many different trees. The sphinx moth can be found from April to October.

Acrea Moth
Wingspan: 1.5 to 2.5" (3.75 to 6.25 cm)

Range: Includes the entire United States

This moth is easy to identify because of its spotted abdomen. A female acrea moth has white hindwings.

Polyphemus Moth
Wingspan: 4 to 6" (10 to 15 cm)

Range: Includes the entire United States

This moth is active at night. It only lives a few days because it does not feed.

Butterflies and Moths Specimen Box

Questions

- Do caterpillars change to butterflies?
- Do larvae change to moths?

Setting the Stage

- Show students a variety of moth and butterfly pictures.
- Ask students if anyone can identify which ones are butterflies and which ones are moths.
- Tell students butterflies and moths look alike. Quite often it is very difficult to tell them apart. Butterflies have bodies which are thin and smooth. Moths have bodies that are fat and furry. It is not easy to observe the bodies of these insects when they are flying in the air. There is another way to distinguish between the two. Look at the antennae. Moths have feathery antennae, and butterflies have club-shaped antennae.
- Ask students to observe the antennae of butterflies in their butterfly books. Point out the smooth edges and the bulb-shaped tips. Continue your lesson with the following activity.

Materials Needed for Each Group

- live caterpillars
- pictures of caterpillars and moths—*Butterfly and Caterpillar* by Barrie Watts (Silver Burdett Company, 1985) is a beautiful collection of color photographs.
- informational books on butterflies and moths
- live moths
- mounted butterflies and moths (optional)
- shoebox
- live plant or leaves
- plastic wrap
- transparent tape
- craft sticks
- data-capture sheet (page 44), one per student

Note to the teacher: Students will construct a home for caterpillars.

Procedure *(Students Instructions)*

1. Cut an opening in the cover of the shoebox. Allow for a 1" (2.5 cm) border around the edge.
2. Cover the opening with plastic wrap. Make sure the edges are securely fastened so that the caterpillar cannot escape.
3. Punch air holes in the end of the shoebox. Do not make them too large.
4. Place the plant or leaves in the box.
5. Go outdoors and look for caterpillars for your specimen boxes. Do not touch the caterpillars with your hands. Use a twig or a craft stick.
6. Change the leaves or remember to water the plant daily. Caterpillars need fresh food.
7. On your data-capture sheet, enter observations and changes for the next several days.

Butterflies and Moths
Specimen Box *(cont.)*

Extensions

- Contact a lepidopterist. Ask him/her to speak to your class. Most collectors are usually honored to speak to children to acquaint them with their hobby or profession.

- Have students do research on the butterfly and moth in history. Many cultures such as the Japanese use pictures of butterflies.

- Have students make butterfly mobiles. They can use pictures in magazines. Mount them and hang them in unusual ways. Encourage students to be creative.

- Have students make butterfly kites. Cut the butterfly shape out of butcher paper or old sheets. Attach string and a tail.

- Plan nature walks. Have students take along their butterfly and moth booklets for identification purposes.

Closure

- Have students add their completed data-capture sheets to their animal journals.

- Have students create posters and make buttons to alert the school population to the plight of the animals of the rain forest.

- Encourage your students to write to the governments where rain forests are located and ask them to stop the destruction of the rain forests. Remind them that the habitat of the butterfly is being destroyed.

Butterflies and Moths
Specimen Box *(cont.)*

Watch your caterpillar daily, record observations, and draw pictures of the various stages it goes through.

BUTTERFLY

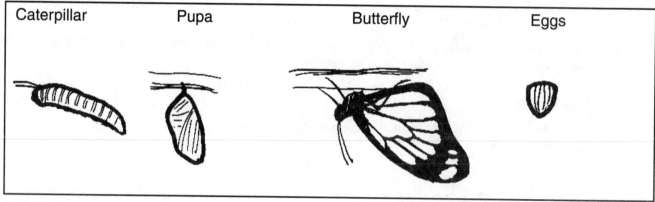

| Caterpillar | Pupa | Butterfly | Eggs |

MOTH

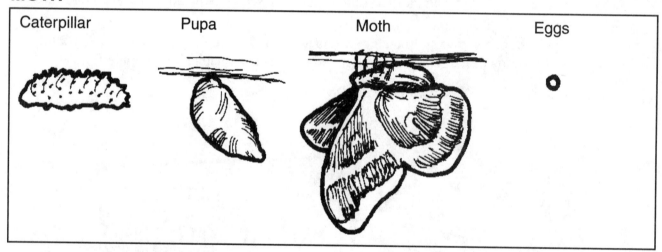

| Caterpillar | Pupa | Moth | Eggs |

NOTES AND OBSERVATIONS:

_____

_____

_____

_____

_____

_____

_____

Bugs That Light the Night

Question

How does a firefly glow?

Setting the Stage

- Tell students that in the rain forest there are some insects that glow in the dark.
- Ask students if they have ever gone out on a spring or summer evening to collect tiny luminescent insects. These tiny creatures fascinate the young and old alike, but just how do these creatures glow?
- Have student do the "Bugs That Light the Night" demonstration to find out.

Materials Needed for Entire Class

- 1/4 tsp (1.25 g) Cypridina (Cypridina are the remains of tiny marine animals which can be obtained from a biology supply house.)
- saliva or water

Procedure *(Student Instructions)*

1. In a room or a closet that is completely dark, place a pinch of Cypridina in the palm of one hand.
2. Using your other hand, add a few drops of water or saliva.
3. With your fingers mix these materials together, using a slight pressure and rotating motion to moisten completely the dried remains of the material.
4. As the material moistens, the Cypridina will glow a bright blue.

Extensions

- Take a class night trip to locate and collect other light-producing organisms. Luminescent mushrooms and other fungi, as well as photobacteria, may be found on rotting logs in some moist areas.
- Marine dinoflagellates and other light-emitting invertebrates may be collected on the beach or in shallow salt water.
- If you do not live near a source of water, some fish in fish markets have some luminescent bacteria on their scales and mucous membranes.

Closure

- In their animal journals, have students record and respond to the following questions: How does a firefly glow? What other organisms might produce their own light? Find and describe some references in literature to the glowworm or firefly.

Just the Facts

You won't find buried treasure or the lost cities of gold in the rain forest, but the rain forests are the most valuable pieces of land on earth. The rain forest's trees and plants are its treasure. In the rain forest green plants take in carbon dioxide and give off oxygen. That is the opposite of what humans do. Humans need oxygen to live.

About eighty percent of what we eat first came from the rain forest. Foods such as bananas come from Southeast Asia. Chocolate is also a product of the rain forest.

In addition to oxygen and food, the rain forest produces about one-fourth the medicines we take to keep healthy. The leaves of the rosy periwinkle are used to treat certain forms of cancer. The plant once grew in the rain forest of Madagascar. Researchers were told about it by the natives who live in the rain forest. So far only one percent of the forest's plants have been examined for their healing powers.

Products such as rubber and diesel oil come from rain forest plants. Rubber from rubber trees is one of the sources of airplane tires and other products. Its heat-resistance quality cannot be duplicated by modern man. Diesel oil comes from the copaiba tree. Its sap is pure diesel oil. As of 1990, twenty percent of Brazil's diesel fuel comes from copaiba.

Knowing how beneficial the rain forests are to mankind makes you wonder why the rain forests are being destroyed each year. About half the world's rain forests have already disappeared, and loggers and ranchers continue to cut down trees and burn land to provide grazing land for cattle. Governments have encouraged poor people to move from crowded cities to practice slash-and-burn farming in the rain forest. Although this is a good method of farming for small groups of people, it is devastating when large groups do it. It is estimated that every year an area about the size of Illinois is destroyed.

Scientists estimate that one species of plant or animal is made extinct every half hour in the rain forest. At that rate, it is predicted that by the middle of the 21st century there will be no more rain forests!

So how can you save the rain forest? You're doing it already. By learning about it and making others aware of the rain forests' importance in the world, we might just be able to save the forests. After all, the cure for many of the world's diseases may reside there.

Where Can We Begin?

Question

Where should we begin when it comes to saving the rain forest?

Setting the Stage

This activity requires some beforehand preparation by the teacher. It has been proven successful in interesting children in ecology because it directly affects their lives.

Prior Preparation

Make a tape recording by someone with a deep, sonorous voice. Have a few minutes of blank tape at the beginning. Record as if the wastepaper basket were talking.

1. Call out several times and ask to be put on the table.
2. Call attention to the kinds of things people are throwing away.
3. Point out the condition of the classroom.
4. Talk about hearing complaints from garbage cans where all the school refuse is dumped.
5. Call attention to Earth as viewed from space. Point out that this is a fragile globe we live on. When it's gone, what do we do?
6. Explain to the children that people are supposed to be consumers, not wasters. Consumers make contributions to the world. Offer to tell them some ways in which they can help.
7. Say, "Mr. or Mrs. (teacher's name) your teacher will tell about the rain forest and how we need to care for it."

Materials Needed for the Class

- classroom wastebasket
- large photograph of Earth taken from space
- tape recorder (battery-operated)
- 90-minute blank recording tape
- *The Great Kapok Tree* by Lynne Cherry
- Save the Rain Forest work sheet (page 49), one for each student.

Procedure

1. Record the tape.
2. Place the tape recorder under the litter in the wastepaper basket in your classroom.
3. Turn it on just before school begins or after lunch or recess.
4. After the tape has played, read the story of *The Great Kapok Tree* to the class.
5. Elicit from the students ways to save the rain forest and write them on the Save the Rain Forest work sheet.

Where Can We Begin? *(cont.)*

Extension

Have the students write and record dialog the plants and animals might say to each other in the rain forest. Short plays or dramatizations could be performed about the environment.

Closure

Have the students research deforestation and write about its impact on mankind.

Where Can We Begin? *(cont.)*

Save The
RAINFORESTS

How Can We Help?

_____

_____

_____

_____

_____

_____

_____

_____

_____

_____

_____

_____

_____

Plan a Poster

Question

How can we make the public aware of what is happening in the rain forest?

Setting the Stage

- Discuss all that the students have learned about the rain forest. Ask the students to brainstorm various ways they can inform the school and the town about what is happening to the world's rain forests.
- Then create posters for display and education.

Materials Needed for Each Individual

- sheet of poster board or a large-size piece of construction paper
- assorted colored markers, crayons, or paints
- pictures and books with plants and animals of the rain forest
- list of threatened, endangered, and extinct plants and animals (page 51)

Procedure

1. Have the students choose a species about which to construct their poster.
2. Divide the poster as shown on the following page.
3. Have the students each create a question for each box about their species. Some examples follow:
   - What does this animal or plant look like?
   - Where does this animal live or plant grow?
   - What usual habits does this animal have?
   - What does this animal or plant eat to survive?
   - What special needs does this animal or plant have?
   - What caused this plant or animal to become endangered?
   - Could humans have prevented this animal or plant from becoming endangered?
   - What can humans do now to save this animal or plant from extinction?
4. Place the posters around school or in local shops around your town.

Extension

Plan a "Rain Forest Awareness Day" to make other students aware of what is happening to our world's rain forests and how they can help save them from extinction. Classroom projects can be shared, and students can present information about what they have learned.

Closure

Write a letter to your local and national governmental agencies to protest the deforestation of the rain forests.

Plan a Poster *(cont.)*

Threatened, Endangered, and Extinct Species

Threatened

These plants or animals are most likely to become endangered due to their numbers, loss of habitat, food supply, or human-induced circumstances.

- Aleutian Canada goose
- alligator
- eastern indigo snake
- leopard darter
- desert tortoise
- valley elderberry
- longhorn beetle
- grizzly bear
- northeastern beach tiger beetle
- Puritan tiger beetle
- Queen Alexandra birdwing *(largest butterfly)*
- noonday snail
- loggerhead sea turtle
- greater sandhill crane
- Shasta salamander
- rough sculpin *(small fish)*
- Trinity bristle snail
- bighorn sheep
- wolverine
- Sierra Nevada red fox
- Little Kern golden trout
- Lalontan cutthroat trout
- Painte cutthroat trout
- San Joaquin antelope
- Swanson's hawk
- Guadalupe fur seal
- Steller's sea lion
- southern sea otter
- southern rubber boa
- black toad
- Cottonball Marsh pupfish

Endangered

These plants and animals are in danger of becoming extinct, gone forever, due to their critically low numbers, loss of habitat, dwindling food supply, and human-induced circumstances.

- badger
- brown pelican
- bullfrog
- California condor
- cheetah
- crocodile
- dolphins
- eagle *(bald* and *golden)*
- elephants *(African* and *Indian)*
- falcon *(peregrine)*
- giant kangaroo rat
- gila monster
- giraffe
- ivory-billed woodpecker
- kangaroo
- kit fox
- loon
- manatee
- mountain lion
- northern spotted owl
- orangutan
- orchid
- panda
- pitcher plant
- polar bear
- sea turtle
- seal *(harp* and *monk)*
- snow leopard
- tigers *(Bengal* and *Siberian)*
- timber wolf
- trumpeter swan
- whales (7 different species)
- whooping crane
- wild mustang
- zebra

Extinct

These plants and animals are extinct, gone forever:

- Alossa fritillary butterfly
- Antioch rubber fly
- Antioch shield-back katydid
- Antioch Spesid wasp
- Clear Lake splittail
- dinosaurs
- dodo bird
- El Segundo flower-loving fly
- long-eared kit fox
- Mono Lake hygratus diving beetle
- oblivious tiger beetle
- Pasadena freshwater shrimp
- passenger pigeon
- saber-toothed tiger
- San Clemente's Bewick's wren
- San Joaquin Valley tiger beetle
- Santa Barbara song sparrow
- sooty crawfish
- Sthenele satyr butterfly
- Stronbeen's Parnassian butterfly
- Tecopa pupfish
- thick-tail chub
- Valley flower-loving fly
- wooly mammoth
- Xerces blue butterfly
- yellow-banded Andrid bee

Make Your Own Paper

Question

How is paper recycled and then reused?

Setting the Stage

- Look in the classroom wastebasket and determine how much paper is thrown away needlessly. Discuss the ways the paper can be resued (e.g., use the backs for scratch paper, cut into small pieces for pads, etc.).
- Making paper will help students understand how paper is recycled and resused.

Materials Needed for the Class

- some newspapers
- water
- bucket or pail
- wire whisk
- three tablespoons cornstarch
- measuring spoons
- rolling pin
- a piece of screen that measures about 6 inches (15 cm) across
- a sheet of plastic wrap large enough to cover the screen

Procedure

*This activity requires a standing time of several hours. Teachers may want to start preparations at the beginning of the day.

1. Tear some newspaper into small pieces.
2. Put the torn paper into the bucket until it is half full.
3. Add enough water to wet the paper pieces thoroughly.
4. Let the paper-and-water mixture stand for several hours.
5. Using the whisk, beat the mixture into a creamy pulp.
6. Dissolve three tablespoons of cornstarch in one cup of water.
7. Add the dissolved cornstarch to the pulp and stir to mix thoroughly.
8. Submerge the piece of screen in the pulp and pull it out.
9. Repeat step 8 until the screen is covered with about 1/8-inch layer of paper pulp.
10. Spread out some sheets of newspaper.
11. Lay the pulp-covered screen on this newspaper.
12. Cover the screen with the sheet of plastic wrap.
13. Using the rolling pin, press out the excess moisture from the pulp.
14. Prop the pulp-covered screen up so that the air can circulate through it and dry it.
15. When the pulp is dry, gently peel this sheet of recycled paper from the screen.

Make Your Own Paper *(cont.)*

Extension

Use your recycled paper to write a poem about the rain forest. Cut the paper into animal or plant shapes and glue them to your poster about the rain forest.

Closure

Have the students investigate who made and used the first paper and what people used before paper. Write this information in your student journal.

Make Your Own Paper *(cont.)*

Directions: Glue a portion of your recycled paper in the space provided and then write a paragraph about the benefits of using recycled paper.

54

Observe

Before beginning your investigation, write your group members' names by their jobs on the lines below.

_____ Expedition Leader _____ Biologist

_____ Stenographer _____ Transcriber

Take a nature walk around the school yard or, if possible, the neighborhood. Take a hand lens, a container that will not harm organisms, and nets. You will be making an observation, which means that you will be using each of your five senses: sight, touch, smell, taste, and sound. How much around you do you really notice?

Write about and draw what you see in the spaces provided on this page.

Write All About It!

_____

_____

_____

_____

_____

_____

_____

_____

_____

Draw It!

Put your finished activity paper in the collection pocket on the side of the table at this station.

Teacher Note: See page 10 for instructions.

Communicate

Before beginning your investigation, write your group members' names by their jobs on the lines below.

_____ Expedition Leader   _____ Biologist

_____ Stenographer   _____ Transcriber

Practice identifying endangered species based on descriptions that other students communicate to you. To do so, first take turns with other groups at this station. One member of your group is to stand facing the rest of the group. Have another member of the group draw an endangered species name from a jar or hat and share it with the rest of the group (except for the student facing you). Note: Sometimes it is best to hang a poster with a description of the endangered species directly behind the student facing the group. In this way, the other members communicating to the student facing them have something to observe and draw from.

The student facing the group is to begin asking the other students relevant questions that will help him/her to deduce the mysterious endangered species. Have the group members answer questions one at a time, rotating from one member to the next. All questions must be answered "Yes," "No," "Sometimes," or "Maybe."

Your teacher will establish guidelines appropriate for your classroom or station situation, such as time allotted or limit to the number of questions asked. Your teacher may also limit or restrict questions about endangered species to biome, predators, prey, and reason for endangerment. Whatever guidelines are established, remember to practice problem-solving techniques—and have some fun doing so!

Sample Questions *(Alligator)*

Do they inhabit a wetland biome? *Yes.*

Are they hunted for their fur? *No.*

Do people fear them? *Sometimes.*

Does this species have a chance of survival? *Maybe.*

Extension

If you prefer to design posters with descriptions as a visual aid, prior to this activity choose an endangered species for each. Be as precise as possible in your illustrations and written descriptions.

Compare

Before beginning your investigation, write your group members' names by their jobs on the lines below.

_____ Expedition Leader   _____ Biologist

_____ Stenographer   _____ Transcriber

Examine the ways freshwater and marine biomes are alike and different. Use the next page, "Earth's Natural Biomes—Water," to determine which organisms exist exclusively in freshwater biomes, which exist exclusively in marine biomes, and which exist in both water biomes. Then fill in the Venn diagram below.

Organisms Inhabiting Both Biomes

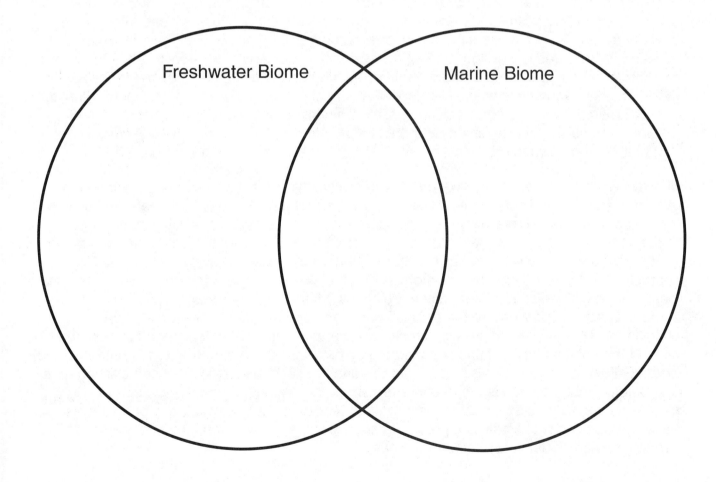

Freshwater Biome   Marine Biome

Put your finished activity paper in the collection pocket on the side of the table at this station.

Compare *(cont.)*

Earth's Natural Biomes—Water

A biome refers to a geographic location or "life zone" on the earth's land or water that is characterized by climatic environmental conditions, such as amount of precipitation, sunlight, humidity, and/or temperature. The specific climate of a biome determines what kinds of plants or animals can survive there. Biomes of the land include coniferous, deciduous, and tropical forests, as well as deserts, tundras, and grasslands. Water biomes are classified as freshwater or marine. Currents, water pressure, and salinity contribute significantly to the organisms that can survive in a given water biome.

Freshwater: Freshwater ecosystems are contained in streams and rivers (running water sources) and lakes and ponds (still-water sources). Water turbidity, dissolved oxygen, suspended particles, temperature, and currents contribute to the survival of a particular species. Flowing water sources contain more dissolved oxygen due to greater mixing with air. However, running water leaves large areas lacking the nutrients required for plankton to survive. Algae and freshwater plants anchor to rocks and pebbles as an adaptation to the water currents. Insect larvae inhabit this location by grasping plants with their hooks or suckers. Where freshwater flow is slow, many plants occupy river or stream banks. Snails, crayfish, and bass are some of the organisms making up the living communities existing there. In lakes and ponds where freshwater is very still, rooted plants are common. Plankton and algae are bountiful, often blocking sunlight from lower depths. Worms, bacteria, and fungi exist in deep, dark regions near the water's bottom. Insects (dragonflies, mosquitoes, and gnats), frogs, fish, birds, and snakes inhabit shores of fresh water biomes.

Marine: Oceans of the world make up 70% of the earth's surface, comprising the greatest variety of species and considered the largest biome of the earth. Light, temperature, salinity level, and water pressure are determining factors as to what organisms will occupy which regions of a marine environment. Light sources dwindle, temperatures decrease, and greater water pressure occurs with increasing depths. Marine biomes are divided into zones characterized by conditions that dictate the forms of life occupying a region. Coasts are located in the littoral zone (areas affected by tides, interfacing with beaches). This shallow zone includes tide-pool organisms (starfish, kelp, and crabs) adaptive to wet and dry conditions. These organisms cling to rocks or burrow in sand. The sublittoral zone extends beyond the continental shelf and is populated by protozoa and algae due to rich nutrients and ideal sunlight exposure. Seals, squids, and turtles are consumers of food webs existing here. The pelagic zone comprises the deeper, darker marine regions. Food is scarce, and conditions are governed by water pressures and lack of light. Bacteria thrive on seafloors. Food chains consist of small fish, predator fish, sharks, and rays. Also, marine mammals (whales and dolphins) inhabit marine biomes.

Order

Before beginning your investigation, write your group members' names by their jobs on the lines below.

_____ Expedition Leader   _____ Biologist

_____ Stenographer   _____ Transcriber

In the food pyramid below, organize each level according to its particular function or role. Begin by arranging, in order, the list of species provided. Complete by labeling each species in its appropriate placement or level on the food pyramid.

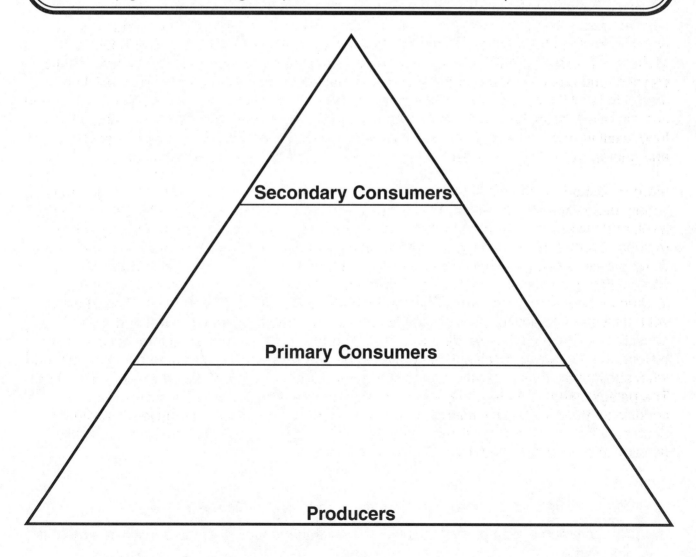

> hawk, spider monkey, toucan, arrow poison frog, boa, morpho butterfly, jaguar, tarantula, green plant leaves, three-toed sloth, tapir, humans

Secondary Consumers

Primary Consumers

Producers

Put your finished activity paper in the collection pocket on the side of the table at this station.

Categorize

Before beginning your investigation, write your group members' names by their jobs on the lines below.

_____ Expedition Leader   _____ Biologist

_____ Stenographer   _____ Transcriber

Place several insect, plant, amphibian, reptile, bird, and mammal species in each of their natural biomes. If organisms exist in two of the given three biomes, place the species' names in the area where the two circles (each representing a given biome) overlap; these regions are designated by sets of numbers. If a species has adapted to the extent that it survives in all three biomes, place the specie's name in the center where all three of the circles (each representing a given biome) overlap. The biomes are numbered as follows:

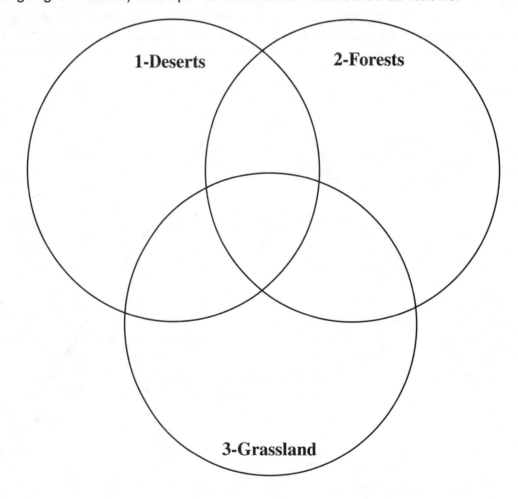

1-Deserts   **2-Forests**

3-Grassland

Answer:

a. What can be said about species living in more than one biome?

b. What are some examples of adaptational traits that enable them to survive in more than one biome?

Put your finished activity paper in the collection pocket on the side of the table at this station.

Categorize *(cont.)*

Earth's Natural Biomes—Land

Coniferous Forest: Cone-bearing trees and shrubs that thrive in cold winters are found in this biome. Bears, elk, deer, moose, lynx, porcupines, squirrels, and many varieties of insects inhabit coniferous forests. Conifers make up about 30% of the world's forests.

Deciduous Forest: Moderate temperatures and precipitation are characteristic of this biome. A variety of broad-leafed trees that lose their leaves annually, such as maple, oak, and beech, form the canopy. The understory (a lower layer of trees) is made by birch, aspen, and pine trees where many insects and birds dwell. The lower levels are formed by shrub-like vegetation, providing food for raccoons, opossum, mice, deer, snakes, and insects. Fallen branches and dead leaves are home to many.

Desert: Prolonged periods of extreme dryness and heat are typical here. Temperatures often exceed 100° F (35° C) during daylight; however, they can drop quickly at night. Xerophytic, drought-tolerant plants, such as cactus and succulents, have adapted to such extreme conditions because their wide-spread root systems tap into the ground water. Owls, vultures, and hawks are some of the predators/scavengers here, reptiles thrive, and tarantulas and scorpions are common. Foxes, rabbits, bats, camels, and mice have learned to adapt to the desert's harshness by requiring less water for survival and by being nocturnal.

Grassland: This biome is characterized by large, open areas of land covered by rich, plush grasses. Typically, summers are warm and winters are cool. Grasslands are located on five continents of the world. They are too moist to become deserts and not rich enough to be forests. Dry winds and brush fires are common to this biome. Zebras, prairie dogs, mice, coyotes, and kangaroos occupy grasslands. Many mammals graze these areas for survival. Hawks and snakes are common consumers.

Rain Forest: Wet, warm, and humid conditions are the norm of this biome. Broad-leaved evergreens, ferns, and orchids are deciduous and make up the forest's layers. The canopy level is usually so dense that little sunlight penetrates to the lower levels, so the floor is covered by fungi and mosses rather than shrubbery. Many exotic birds and monkeys live in the canopies. At lower levels, insects are abundant. Various species of snakes, lizards, and other reptiles are common, and eagles, jaguars, and leopards are predators of the small game.

Tundra: Mostly cold and dry conditions characterize this biome. Days are long in summer, and in winter brief daylight is typical. Plants grow close to the ground where temperatures are warmest and protection from the frigid winds is greatest. The plants include mosses, lichens, and short, flowering plants which have adapted to life in areas covered by snow most of the year. Many birds such as fowl, geese, ducks, and gulls nest in the low-lying vegetation. In the summer the snow slightly melts, leaving a soggy ground. As winter approaches, the birds migrate south. Caribou, polar bears, hares, foxes, wolves, and owls are inhabitants of tundra regions. These animals have adapted to the harsh conditions by producing warm furs and by having natural camouflage.

Relate

Before beginning your investigation, write your group members' names by their jobs on the lines below.

_____ Expedition Leader   _____ Biologist

_____ Stenographer   _____ Transcriber

Match what each scientist studies:

1. Botanist
2. Entomologist
3. Zoologist
4. Paleontologist
5. Biologist
6. Meteorologist
7. Oceanographer
8. Geologist
9. Chemist
10. Physicist
11. Astronomer
12. Ecologist

A. Studies marine life and environments
B. Studies animals
C. Studies plants
D. Studies the molecular structure of matter
E. Studies insects
F. Studies the weather and climate
G. Studies fossils
H. Studies the interrelations of living things and their environment
I. Studies the planets and stars
J. Studies rocks and minerals
K. Studies forces and energy
L. Studies relationships of living things to one another

What science would you like to study? Explain why!

Put your finished activity paper in the collection pocket on the side of the table at this station.

Teacher Key *(cover before duplicating):* 1. C; 2. E; 3. B; 4. G; 5. L; 6. F; 7. A; 8. J; 9. D; 10. K; 11. I; 12. H

Infer

Before beginning your investigation, write your group members' names by their jobs on the lines below.

_____ Expedition Leader   _____ Biologist

_____ Stenographer   _____ Transcriber

To help understand and learn the skill of problem solving, we sometimes have to organize, interpret, analyze, and evaluate information and then make an inference based on the data collected. Data can help us recognize patterns so that we can reasonably predict or forecast trends and possible occurrences. Oftentimes, enough random data can help us establish norms, thereby determining the probability of the occurrence based on past results.

Fact: Life forms on land were prevented from beginning until plants had produced enough oxygen to create the ozone layer—the natural protective layer of the atmosphere which blocks out and absorbs the harmful energy of the sun (mainly, ultraviolet radiation). This process took billions of years to create the right conditions for supporting life forms on land. Due to pollution, the ozone layer is beginning to deplete, and there has been mass destruction of plant life. If these conditions continue, what can we infer? Answer here.

_____

_____

_____

_____

_____

_____

_____

_____

_____

_____

Put your finished activity paper in the collection pocket on the side of the table at this station.

Apply

Before beginning your investigation, write your group members' names by their jobs on the lines below.

_____ Expedition Leader   _____ Biologist

_____ Stenographer   _____ Transcriber

Working with your group, brainstorm what you might suggest to each of the organisms below to help them survive under current circumstances. Be sure to record in your journal your responses to each, and indicate your thoughts as to whether or not each will adapt, either by changing its behavior or changing physically. Are any likely to become extinct? Why? Also in your group, come up with three additional scenarios to share with the class.

Recently, natural predators have been introduced to the biome I inhabit. It is more difficult to avoid danger. When I search for food and roam around in the open, I risk my survival. What should I do?

I live in the canopies of rain forests and have always felt protected and provided for. However, more and more of my habitat around me is being destroyed. My home is becoming overpopulated by species forced to leave their homes. I am in fear that I, too, will be homeless one day. What should I do?

I have come to realize that my entire existence is threatened due to something I possess that man considers a rare and valuable commodity. Thousands of my friends and family have been hunted for their fur or tusks. What can be done to prevent our extinction?

I am told that I am a dreadful and ferocious creature. Many have stated that I do not deserve to live. I only do what is natural. I want to carry on my species and to exist in a kind, unaltered environment. However, my species is threatened due to man's fear of me. If they only understood that all I want is to survive and to follow my instincts. What is in store for me?

Competition for food in the biome in which I live is becoming greater, and I am limited in choices since I tend to stay low to the ground and am unable to climb. There is much food way up in the tall trees, but I cannot wait until it falls naturally. How am I going to eat, and where will I get food for my young?

Some organisms in my environment have dwindled in numbers because humans consider them pests or menaces. However, I rely on them for food, and without this nutrition I will surely become threatened as well. What shall I do?

Animal Information Cards

Guide to Using the Cards

Pages 65–75 are filled with Animal Information Cards. These boxes may be mounted on colored construction paper and be placed on the classroom walls. Pages 76–78 have the corresponding Animal Illustration Cards. These may also be mounted and displayed adjacent to the appropriate Information Cards.

The Animal Information and Illustration Cards can also be used in a matching game. For example, post the information cards around the room. Read the descriptions, one at a time, to the class. Allow one student to match the correct illustration to the Information Card.

These cards can provide an excellent, initial resource if you are having your students do animal research reports. At the end of this section, there are some blank cards for other rain forest animals.

Challenge: The following are challenge questions and activities related to some selected animals on the Animal Information Cards. You might use these as extra credit, quiz questions, or discussion starting points.

Parrots: Research how parrots can be bred humanely in captivity. Would you buy for a pet a parrot bred this way? Why or why not?

Harpy Eagle: Being a predator, the harpy eagle is an integral part of the balance of nature in the tropical rain forest. What do you think would happen if this predator became extinct?

Sloth: If a sloth moves through the branches at only one-half mile per hour, how long would it take for him to travel to the next cecropia tree six miles away?

Jaguar: Compare and contrast the plight of the jaguar with that of the leopard.

Chimpanzees: Write a commercial for a tool from a chimp's point of view. Perform your commercial for your class.

Quetzal

The quetzal of Southern Mexico and Central America is among the most beautiful birds in the world. The quetzal is also known as the royal bird of Costa Rica. Its body is green with highlights of gold and red. The black wings of the quetzal have splashes of white on them. The male quetzal is about 15 inches (38 cm) in length from head to tail. However, the long wisp of feathers beneath its tail add another 15 to 30 inches (38 to 76 cm) to the quetzal's length. The female quetzal is slightly less attractive. Her feathers are not as vibrant in color nor are her feathers as long and graceful as her male counterpart's.

Quetzals are known to eat ants and wasps, but they mainly depend on the fruits of the wild avocado tree for nourishment. The quetzal is an endangered animal because excessive logging of the rain forest has resulted in the loss of many wild avocado trees.

The quetzal's great beauty has inspired people to incorporate it into their cultures in many ways. Often, rain forest native art and mythology have featured this royal bird. The ancient Mayans and Aztecs considered the quetzal to be a sacred creature. Today, the quetzal serves as the national symbol of Guatemala.

Animal Information Cards *(cont.)*

Macaw

Macaws are the world's largest parrots. There are several different kinds of spectacularly colored macaws, and they all live in South America. Macaws are seed predators rather than seed dispersers. They are able to eat the toughest fruits and seeds, even if they contain toxic chemicals.

Macaws have large, powerful bodies which protect them from being eaten by many bird predators. The macaw's hooked beak can open even the hardest nuts, like Brazil nuts, with ease. It uses the edge of the beak like a saw to cut partially through the shell, making it easy to complete the job. The top and bottom parts of the macaw's beak constantly rub against each other, keeping the edges sharp.

The macaw's beak is also useful as an extra foot when climbing through the trees. The macaw's foot has four toes. Two of these face forward, and two of them face backward. This enables the macaws to pick up objects and hold them tightly.

Parrots, such as macaws, make popular pets and are often taken into captivity. Although there are laws attempting to protect the parrots, poachers continue to illegally capture and sell these beautiful creatures.

Toucan

Some of the most distinctive birds that come from the tropical rain forests are toucans. Toucans have large, brightly colored beaks which are serrated and are displayed in courtship rituals. Toucan beaks are so large that they are sometimes longer than the toucan's body!

There are about 37 species of toucans, the largest of which is the Ramphastos. In general, the toucan's body is usually one to two feet (30 to 60 cm) in length. The plumage of these birds matches their personalities; both are very loud. Sections of the vibrant colors such as red, yellow, and green contrast sharply with the mostly black or dark green feathers on the toucan's body. These colorful birds are supported by strong legs and feet which have two toes pointed forward and two toes pointed backward.

Toucans nest in the tree cavities of the Central and South American rain forests. In these nests, both toucan parents incubate and raise their offspring. Fruit makes up the bulk of the toucan diet.

Animal Information Cards *(cont.)*

Harpy Eagle

The topical rain forest is the home to the world's largest and most ferocious eagle, the harpy eagle. This rare predator hunts high up in the jungle canopy. It sleeps at night and hunts by day. The harpy eagle is a very swift and agile flyer which enables it to chase monkeys through the jungle. Its gray feathers provide the eagle with a natural camouflage.

The harpy eagle makes its nest in the tallest emergent trees (most often the silk cotton trees). Usually only one harpy eagle chick is successfully raised on the large platform of twigs used as a nest. It takes six months for the chick to reach adulthood.

The harpy eagle dines mainly on unsuspecting, sleeping sloths and chattering capuchin monkeys. Occasionally, their diet includes agouti, kinkajous, snakes, anteaters, large parrots, and small deer.

Caiman

Caimans are reptiles that are closely related to their Central and South American neighbors, the alligators. Adult caimans are usually four to six feet (1.8 m) in length. They have short legs and powerful tails which are used for both swimming and as weapons.

Caimans live along riverbanks where they patiently wait for thirsty animals to come for a drink—then, they attack their unsuspecting prey! They can float under the water with only their eyes, nostrils, and ears showing. A valve closes off the gullet of the windpipe so that the mouth can be opened under water to eat its favorite food—fish. The caiman's greatest enemy is man.

Some caimans have been found to leave the river to lay their eggs next to termite nests. As the termites continue to build their nests, they surround the caiman's eggs. The nests keep half the eggs warm and half the eggs cool. The warm eggs develop into male caimans, and the cool eggs develop into females. When the baby caimans hatch, they head straight for the river where they spend their lives.

Animal Information Cards *(cont.)*

Gorilla

Because gorillas are the largest living primates, they are quite often misunderstood. They are usually represented as aggressive, violent, and short-tempered creatures, when in fact they are actually among the most gentle primates in existence. These giants of the African rain forests can reach up to six feet (180 cm) in height and 400 pounds (180 kg) in weight. Despite their size, fighting among the gorillas is rare.

Contrary to popular belief, the gorillas are not carnivores (meat eaters), but rather they are herbivores (plant eaters). During the daytime they forage for food on the forest floor. Unlike other members of the ape family, most gorillas, due to their size, do not scour the treetops in search of food or shelter.

Gorillas live and travel in family groupings. The family unit consists of one dominate silverback male (the term "silverback" comes from the gray fur on a mature male), one or two females, a few young males, and various juveniles. Gorillas are quadrupeds because they travel on all four limbs. They use the knuckles of their hands to help support their heavy upper bodies.

Tarsier

The tarsier lives in the rain forests of Indonesia, Malaysia, Brunei, and the Philippines. This Southeast Asian mammal is in danger of extinction because its forests are being destroyed. The tarsier is a rat-sized relative of the monkey.

This creature is one of the strangest looking primates, in large part because of its unique eyes, ears, and feet. Its body is only about six inches (15 cm) in length. The tarsier has long, powerful hind legs which allow it to leap up to 20 feet (6 meters). The pads on their toes and fingers help them to hold onto branches. The tarsier's head can almost turn in a complete circle. This is a very important feature since the tarsier cannot move its eyes.

This animal spends most of its life living in the trees of the rain forest. It is, for the most part, nocturnal (active during the night and resting during the day), and it has large, sharp eyes that enable it to hunt all sorts of small animals at night. It leaps onto its prey (which is usually a lizard or an insect), it catches the creature with its hands, and then kills it with its sharp teeth.

Animal Information Cards *(cont.)*

Fer-de-Lance

The most feared poisonous snake found in Central and South America is called the fer-de-lance. This snake gets its name from the Creole-French language, and it means "head of a lance." A lance is a type of weapon that has a spearhead, which some people believe looks similar to the head of this snake. The fer-de-lance averages four to six feet (1.2 to 1.8 meters) in length but can grow up to seven feet (2.1 meters) long. Usually olive or dark brown in color, it has a pattern of dark-edged triangles on its skin.

Small depressions on its head mark a heat-sensing organ that helps the animal find its warm-blooded, mammalian prey by the heat the prey generates. The fer-de-lance protects itself by striking its enemy. Its venom quickly produces severe hemorrhaging and is lethal.

This snake lives in the understory or forest floor, hiding among the leaf litter, tree roots, and buttresses. It gives birth to live offspring and may produce as many as 70 young at one time.

Boa

Boas are nonpoisonous snakes. They kill their food by wrapping themselves around animals and squeezing tightly until the animals die from suffocation. Boas then stretch their jaws open extremely wide to swallow their prey whole. They are able to open their jaws so wide that they can actually swallow animals that are larger than their own heads.

There are about 70 species in the boa family which can be found worldwide. Unlike some other types of snakes who lay eggs, the boa gives birth to live offspring. Some kinds of boas never grow any longer than 24 inches (61 cm), while others, such as the boa constrictor, may grow as large as 14 feet (4 meters) in length.

One of the most beautiful snakes found in Central and South America is the emerald tree boa. Its green skin is striped with white or yellow, which camouflages it well in its home in the canopy layer. This protective coloration allows the snake to approach its prey without being seen and also helps it to avoid being eaten by its predators, one of which is the harpy eagle.

Animal Information Cards *(cont.)*

Lemur

Lemurs are distant cousins of monkeys. They are found only on the island of Madagascar. They have been able to survive there because of a lack of monkeys on the island that would be competing for the same food.

There are 15 different kinds of lemurs in Madagascar. Most of them are cat- or squirrel-sized but some, like the mouse lemur, are as small as five inches (12.5 cm) long and weigh only two ounces (56 g). The indri lemur is the biggest lemur, growing to over two feet (61 m) long. It is able to make extraordinary leaps through the trees but, when on the ground, bounces on its big back legs.

Most lemurs roam the forest in small groups looking for food. They eat fruit, leaves, bark, and insects. Different types of lemurs are active during different times of the day. Some species are nocturnal (active at night), some are diurnal (active during the day), and some are active only at dusk.

The lemur population is dwindling. Some species of lemurs are in danger of extinction because the forests of Madagascar are rapidly being destroyed.

Aye-aye

The cat-sized aye-aye is an unusual and rare type of lemur. Its enormous eyes and rounded, hairless ears indicate that the aye-aye is nocturnal (it comes out at night). During the daytime it sleeps in hollow trees or among branches. The aye-aye is a very small animal, measuring only about 36 inches (.91 m) long; more than half of that length is due to its bushy tail.

The aye-aye is a loner. It hunts alone, using its long fingers to scoop out bamboo pith, sugar cane, beetles, and insect larvae. The curved, slender fingers are also used to comb its fur. Unfortunately for the aye-aye, the natives of Madagascar believe that these long fingers possess magical properties and bring good luck to the owners. Many aye-ayes have lost their lives because of this—their fingers did not bring them good luck!

Aye-ayes can be found only on the island of Madagascar, and there are fewer than 10 aye-ayes known to exist there. Aye-ayes are not found in any of the world's zoos; therefore, the only way we will probably ever view one is to look in a book.

Animal Information Cards *(cont.)*

Orangutan

Orangutans can be found only on the islands of Borneo and Sumatra in Southeast Asia. They were named "men of the woods" because their faces are so human-looking. Orangutans are wonderful climbers and spend most of their time in the treetops, swinging from branch to branch.

Like other apes, orangutans do not have tails. They have long, red hair and strong arms. Their long toes help them grip the branches as they climb in the trees.

Orangutans have huge appetites. Their favorite food is fruit, but they will also eat leaves, shoots, tree bark and, occasionally, birds' eggs. Orangutans are very clever and have learned to follow fruit-eating birds to find their favorite food.

The orangutans have become very rare due to the loss of their habitat, the rain forest. Additionally, orangutans have been hunted, captured, and sold as pets. Special reserves have been set up to help the remaining orangutans survive.

Indian Elephant

Indian elephants are the largest animals in the rain forests of Asia, although their African cousins are larger. Elephants roam about in small herds. Their diet mainly consists of leaves which they pull from the trees and shove into their mouths by using their trunks.

The Indian elephant's two very large teeth are called tusks. These tusks consist of ivory. The females usually have smaller tusks than the males. Unlike the flat back of the African elephant, the Indian elephant has a strongly arched back. It has a domed forehead and a smooth trunk. It can weigh up to six tons (5.44 tonnes). The ears of the Indian elephant do not reach down as far as its mouth and are smaller than the ears of the African elephant.

Indian elephants have been trained as workers in the forests. They are better than machines when it comes to getting out big logs from between the trees. They can drag huge logs from the forest and pick them up with their trunks and tusks. The forests where they live are gradually being destroyed, and the irony of it is that the tamed, working elephants are helping to cause the damage.

Animal Information Cards *(cont.)*

Anteater

This tree-living, cat-sized anteater is also called a tamandua. It has short, coarse fur and a prehensile tail. South American tamanduas have honey-colored coats, while the Central American ones have bold, two-toned black and tan coats.

The tamandua has powerful claws that help it both in climbing and in getting food. It wraps its tail around tree limbs to hold on while it rips open ant and termite nests with its claws. It then catches the insects with its long sticky tongue, licking up thousands at one time. It also will eat other insects such as bees and beetles.

Contrary to common belief, the anteater does not eat all types of ants or termites! It avoids army ants because they are too aggressive and can sting. It also will not eat leaf-cutter ants as they are spiny and difficult to swallow in its long, toothless mouth. Azteca ants are a favorite of the tamandua, but the anteaters approach these nests very cautiously. After several minutes of eating these Azteca ants, thousands more of them pour out from the nest, covering the tamandua and biting it with their tiny jaws, causing the tamandua to retreat.

Agouti

The agouti is a large, rabbit-sized rodent with a short tail and long legs. It is mainly active by day (diurnal) but is also active at dusk or at night (nocturnal). It lives on the forest floor and sleeps in burrows.

Agoutis have a very strange behavior called scatter-hoarding. Most rodents destroy all the seeds that they gather and eat; the agouti, however, carries seeds long distances and buries them whole.

There are some trees that produce seeds that are too heavy to be dispersed by bats or monkeys and have to rely on animals like agoutis for dispersal. Brazil nut fruits fall to the ground where their hard, woody shells are chiseled open by the agouti.

The agouti eats some of the seeds and scatter-hoard the rest. They do not usually find all the Brazil nut seeds that they bury; consequently, these seeds germinate and grow into new Brazil nut trees.

Animal Information Cards *(cont.)*

Sloth

The sloth does nearly everything upside down. Found in Central and South America, this slowest-of-all-mammals' top speed is one-half mile per hour. It lives its entire life in one cecropia tree, hanging by its huge hook-like claws. In addition to cecropia leaves, it eats flowers, fruit, and insects.

Its long, coarse, grayish-brown fur grows from its belly towards it back (the opposite of all other animals' fur), which enables the rain to run off easily, keeping the sloth dry in the wet rain forest. Nonetheless, its fur often appears a greenish color due to the algae that grow on it. In addition to the algae, the sloth's fur contains sloth moths, beetles, and mites. When the sloth descends to the forest floor, these insects utilize the sloth's dung to lay their eggs. Caterpillars also live on the sloth's fur and feed on the algae.

The sloth spends nearly its entire life among the tree's branches. It visits the forest floor about once every week or two to defecate, thereby fertilizing its own home. Once on the ground, the sloth cannot walk and must drag itself. However, during the rainy season, when the Amazon floods, sloths can swim from treetop to treetop.

Jaguar

The rarely seen jaguar is the largest predator of the dense forests of Central and South America. The jaguar is an excellent swimmer and climber and usually can be found close to water where it sleeps by day and hunts by night (a nocturnal animal). It prefers to eat large animals like wild pig or tapir, but, being an excellent hunter, its diet also includes sloths, snakes, mice, caimans, turtles, iguanas, and fish. The jaguar is the major predator of the lower levels of the rain forest.

The jaguar's coat is spotted like its cousin's, the leopard, but its rings are different. Nearly all of them have a spot in the middle. This camouflages the jaguar as he stalks through the jungle. Jaguars can weigh up to three hundred pounds (136 kg).

A number of disasters threaten these beautiful creatures. Jaguars have long been hunted for their luxurious fur. Although there are many laws protecting these creatures, illegal killing and smuggling of the jaguars' fur continues. As the population grows, rain forest land is being slashed and burned to clear land for ranching. This is causing a loss of habitat for many rain forest animals which the jaguar depends upon for food. Consequently, the jaguars have begun to feed on the ranchers' livestock. In turn, this has resulted in their being killed by the ranchers.

Animal Information Cards *(cont.)*

Chimpanzee

Scientists believe that of all wild animals, chimpanzees are our closest relatives. Chimpanzees make their homes in the rain forests of Africa. They have been known to live in groups of up to 100 animals. The noisiest male is usually the group leader. Male chimpanzees often fight with one another. Female chimps are friendlier and get along well. Male chimps grow to be about five feet (1.52 m) tall and weigh about 110 pounds (50 kg). Female chimps are usually a little smaller. Chimps, like other apes, do not have tails.

Chimpanzees eat plants and meat. They are capable of killing pigs and antelope for food. Male chimps work in teams to trap monkeys in trees. When they are lucky enough to find a large amount of food, the males make drumming noises on the tree trunks to call other chimps to the feast.

Chimpanzees are very clever. They have learned how to use simple tools to get the food they want. They use sticks to crack nuts to get the juicy kernels inside and to catch tasty termites. Chimps have also been known to chew leaves, making them spongy, so they can use them to soak up water for drinking.

_____

(animal)

_____

_____

_____

_____

_____

_____

_____

Blank Cards

(animal)

Animal Illustration Cards

Quetzal

Macaw

Toucan

Harpy Eagle

Caiman

Gorilla

Animal Illustration Cards *(cont.)*

Tarsier

Fer-de-Lance

Boa

Lemur

Aye-aye

Orangutan

Animal Illustration Cards *(cont.)*

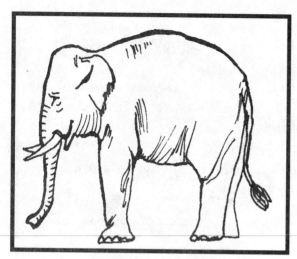

Indian Elephant

Anteater

Agouti

Sloth

Jaguar

Chimpanzee

Science Safety

Discuss the necessity for science safety rules. Reinforce the rules on this page or adapt them to meet the needs of your classroom. You may wish to reproduce the rules for each student or post them in the classroom.

Note to the Teacher: When doing any plant collection, be sure to caution your students to collect only in permitted areas and to do so gently, not harming the plants in any way. They should also know how to recognize the poisonous plants in your area and know not to touch the parts of the plants about which they are uncertain. Warn them not to eat the parts of any plants they collect in the wild, unless they have been assured of their safety by a knowledgeable adult.

Animals also deserve the same respect and care. In handling any animal, students must first learn the proper way to hold it and respond to it, if any touch at all is appropriate.

1. Begin science activities only after all directions have been given.

2. Never put anything in your mouth unless it is required by the science experience.

3. Always wear safety goggles when participating in any lab experience.

4. Dispose of waste and recyclables in proper containers.

5. Follow classroom rules of behavior while participating in science experiences.

6. Review your basic class safety rules everytime you conduct a science experience.

You can have fun and still be safe at the same time!

Rain Forest Journal

Rain forest journals are an effective way to integrate science and language arts. Students are to record their observations, thoughts, and questions about past science experiences in a journal to be kept in the science area. The observations may be recorded in sentences or sketches which keep track of changes both in the science item or in the thoughts and discussions of the students.

Rain forest journal entries can be completed as a team effort or an individual activity. Be sure to model the making and recording of observations several times when introducing the journals to the science area.

Use the student recordings in the rain forest journals as a focus for class science discussions. You should lead these discussions and guide students with probing questions, but it is usually not necessary for you to give any explanation. Students come to accurate conclusions as a result of classmates' comments and your questioning. Rain forest journals can also become part of the students' portfolios and overall assessment program. Journals are valuable assessment tools for parent and student conferences as well.

How to Make a Rain Forest Journal

1. Cut two pieces of 8.5 " x 11" (22 cm x 28 cm) construction paper to create a cover. Reproduce page 81 and glue it to the front cover of the journal. Allow students to draw pictures of endangered species in the box on the cover.
2. Insert several rain forest journal pages. (See page 82.)
3. Staple the pages together and cover the stapled edge with book tape.

My
Rain Forest
Journal

Name _____

Rain Forest Journal

Illustration

This is what happened: _____

_____

_____

_____

_____

This is what I learned: _____

_____

_____

_____

_____

My Science Activity

K-W-L Strategy

Answer each question about the topic you have chosen.

Topic: _____

K—What I already **know:**_____

_____

_____

_____

_____

W—What I **want to find out:** _____

_____

_____

_____

_____

L—What I **learned after doing the activity**:_____

_____

_____

_____

_____

Investigation Planner *(Option 1)*

Observation

_____

_____

Question

_____

_____

Hypothesis

_____

_____

Procedure

Materials Needed:

_____

_____

_____

_____

Step-by-Step Directions: (Number each step.)

_____

_____

_____

_____

_____

_____

Investigation Planner *(Option 2)*

Science Experience Form

Scientist _____

Title of Activity _____

Observation: What caused us to ask the question?

_____

_____

_____

Question: What do we want to find out?

_____

_____

_____

Hypothesis: What do we think we will find out?

_____

_____

_____

Procedure: How will we find out? (List step by step.)

_____

_____

_____

Results: What actually happened?

_____

_____

_____

Conclusions: What did we learn?

_____

_____

Rain Forest Observation Area

In addition to station-to-station activities, students should be given other opportunities for real-life science experiences. For example, a minicomputer and terrarium can provide vehicles for discovery learning if students are given enough time and space to observe them.

Set up a rain forest observation area in your classroom. As children visit this area during open work time, expect to hear stimulating conversations and questions among them. Encourage curiosity but respect their independence!

Books with facts pertinent to the subject, item, or process being observed should be provided for students who are ready to research more sophisticated information.

Sometimes it is very stimulating to set up a science experiment or add something interesting to the rain forest observation area without a comment from you at all. If the experiment or materials in the observation area should not be disturbed, reinforce with students the need to observe without touching or picking up.

Assessment Forms

The following chart can be used by the teacher to rate cooperative learning groups in a variety of settings.

Science Groups Evaluation Sheet

Room: _____   Date: _____

Activity: _____

Everyone

. . . gets started.

. . . participates.

. . . knows jobs.

. . . solves group problems.

. . . cooperates.

. . . keeps noise down.

. . . encourages others.

Group									
1	2	3	4	5	6	7	8	9	10

Teacher Comment

_____

Bragging rights for the group session: _____

_____

Assessment Forms *(cont.)*

The evaluation form below provides student groups with the opportunity to evaluate the group's overall success.

Cooperative Group Evaluation

Assignment: _____

Date: _____

Scientists	Jobs
_____	_____
_____	_____
_____	_____
_____	_____

As a group, decide which face you should fill in and complete the remaining sentences.

1. We finished our assignment on time, and we did a good job.
2. We encouraged each other, and we cooperated with each other.

3. We did best at _____

_____

4. Next time we could improve at_____

_____

Assessment Forms *(cont.)*

The following form may be used as part of the assessment process for hands-on science experiences.

Science Anecdotal Record Form

Date:_____

Scientist's Name: _____

Topic: _____

Assessment Situation: _____

Instructional Task: _____

Behavior/Skill Observed: _____

_____

_____

_____

_____

This behavior/skill is important because: _____

_____

_____

_____

_____

Super Biologist Award

This is to certify that

_____
Name

made a science discovery.

Congratulations!

_____
Teacher

_____
Date

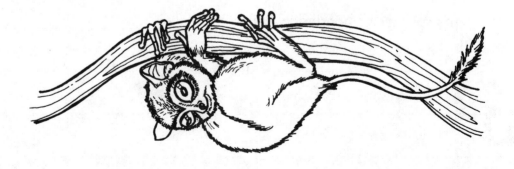

90

Glossary

adaptation—Changes in the behavior or structure of plants or animals that enable them to survive in their surroundings.

agroforestry—A land-use system in which trees and crops are grown alongside each other. This maintains the forest as a self-renewing resource.

algae—A group of simple plants that usually live in wet and damp places. Many of them are very small.

anthropologist—A person who studies the physical and social characteristics of mankind.

biodiversity—Many different kinds of life in one area.

biome—The largest type of ecological unit, characterized by a distinctive set of plants and animals maintained under the climatic conditions of the region. Examples include deserts and tropical rain forests.

bromeliad—A tropical plant that grows on the branches or trunks of trees. It is a member of the pineapple family.

buttress—On some of the tall rain forest trees a fan-shaped bottom that helps hold the tree upright.

camouflage—The way in which animals avoid the attention of their enemies by resembling or blending in with their surroundings.

canopy—A thick, overhead layer of the rain forest formed by the branches and leaves of the tall trees.

carbon dioxide—A colorless gas that is formed by the combustion and decomposition of organic substances. Carbon dioxide is absorbed from the air by plants in photosynthesis.

cash crops—Agricultural products, such as coffee or bananas, that are sold for profit, often by export, rather than raised for consumption by the producer.

clear cutting—Removing all the trees in a forest, leaving an open patch.

conservation—Protection of natural resources from waste or loss or harm.

decomposer—Organisms, such as bacteria, fungi, and many insects, that break down dead plant and animal materials to be recycled and used by the living.

deforestation—The destruction of a forest. In the tropics, deforestation is caused by a number of activities, such as slash-and-burn agriculture, cattle ranching, and timber harvesting.

development—The alteration of the environment for the benefit of human beings.

diurnal—Refers to animals that are active during the day and rest at night.

drip tips—Leaves that come to a point, allowing rainwater to drip off.

Glossary

echolocation—The ability of an animal such as a bat or a dolphin to orient itself by the reflection of the sound it produces.

ecology—The study of the environment and the relationship of organisms to it.

ecosystem—A community of animals, plants, and microscopic life that interact in a particular place in the environment.

emergent—The layer of trees in the rain forest that towers in height above others and receives the most sunlight. They can grow to be 300 feet (91 meters) tall.

endangered species—An animal or plant that is threatened with extinction.

environment—All the physical surroundings that are around a person, animal, or plant.

epiphyte—A plant that grows on another plant but does not harm it.

equator—An artificial circle that splits the earth into the northern and southern hemispheres.

erosion—Washing or wearing away of soil.

ethnobotanist—A researcher who studies native plants and their use by the local, indigenous peoples.

exploitation—To use for some purpose for one's own advantage or profit at someone or something else's expense.

extinction—The permanent loss of an animal or plant species.

food chain—The flow of energy (food) among different groups of organisms in a natural community.

forest floor—The bottom layer of the rain forest.

global—A term pertaining to the planet Earth, meaning worldwide or universal.

greenhouse effect—The trapping of heat by the air around the earth.

habitat—An area that provides enough food, water, shelter, and space for an organism to survive and reproduce.

humidity—The amount of water vapor in the air.

hunter-gatherers—People who get most or all of the food they need by hunting and by gathering wild plants.

indigenous—Growing or living naturally in a particular region or environment. The term "indigenous people" is used to mean native people.

invertebrates—A group of animals that have no backbone.

jungle—A general term which is interchangeable with the term "tropical rain forest."

E

F

G

H

I

J

Glossary (cont.)

L
M
N

liana—A woody vine that is rooted in the soil and grows up tree trunks or in open areas.

mammal—Any animal that feeds its babies with milk from the mother's body.

nature reserve—An area set aside to protect wild plants and animals, often rare ones, that are in danger of becoming extinct.

nectar—A sugary fluid secreted by plants to attract pollinators.

nocturnal—Refers to animals that are active at night and rest during the day.

nutrients—Substances such as vitamins and minerals that are necessary for life.

O

organic—Of plant or animal origin.

oxygen—A gas that is given off by plants and used by animals.

ozone layer—The region of concentrated ozone that shields the earth from excessive ultraviolet radiation.

P

parasite—An organism dependent upon another living organism for support or existence.

photosynthesis—A process in which plants convert carbon dioxide into water and sugar.

pollen—Powder-like microspores produced by the flower, containing the male sex cell.

pollination—The transfer of pollen from the male reproductive organs to the female in seed plants.

predator—An animal that hunts or traps other animals for food.

prey—An animal that is caught and eaten by a predator.

R

rain forest—A very dense forest in a region, usually tropical, where rain is very heavy throughout the year.

reforestation—The action of renewing forest cover by planting seeds or young trees.

resource—A product of the environment which has use or value.

S

seed dispersal—The way that seeds travel from the parent plant to the ground by wind, gravity, or animals.

slash-and-burn agriculture—The method of agriculture in which people clear land by cutting down patches of forest and burning the debris.

soil erosion—The washing away of soil by wind and water due to the lack of protection of the thin layer of top soil.

species—A group of organisms that have the same traits and can produce offspring that can also produce offspring.

sustainable development—Development that uses natural resources in an efficient way and without destroying the basis of their productivity. It allows natural resources to regenerate.

Glossary *(cont.)*

T

threatened species—Any species of indigenous plant or animal that could become endangered in the near future if the factors causing its population decline are not reversed.

topsoil—The surface soil, including the organic layer where plants have most of their roots.

tropical—Hot, humid zone between the Tropic of Cancer and the Tropic of Capricorn.

tropical rain forest—An evergreen forest located at low elevations in regions between the Tropic of Cancer and the Tropic of Capricorn. Tropical rain forests are characterized by abundant rainfall and a very warm, humid climate year round.

U

understory—The layer growing under the canopy. This layer is comprised of shrubs, herbs, and young trees.

V

vertebrates—The group of animals which have internal skeletons with backbones.

Bibliography

Academic American Encyclopedia, *Jungle.* Vol.11. Groiler Inc., 1986.

Amery, Heather. *The Know-How Book of Experiments.* Usborne Publishing Ltd., 1977.

Althea. *Rainforest Homes.* Cambridge U Pr., 1985.

Burnie, David. *How Nature Works: 100 Ways Parents & Kids Can Share the Secrets of Nature.* Reader's Digest, 1991.

Cherry, Lynne. *The Great Kapok Tree: A Tale of the Amazon Rain Forest.* Harcourt Brace Jovanovich, 1990.

Chinery, Michael. *Rainforest Animals.* Random Bks Yng Read, 1992.

Cooper, Sally Ann and Cradler, Carolyn. *General Science.* Media Materials, 1988.

Costa de Beauregard, Diane. *Animals in Jeopardy.* Young Discovery Library, 1991.

Cuthbert, Susan. *Endangered Creatures.* Lion USA, 1992.

De Vito, Alfred and Krockover, Gerald. *Creative Sciencing: Ideas for Teachers & Children Grades K to Eight*. Addison-Wesley, 1991.

EarthWorks Group. *50 Simple Things Kids Can Do To Save the Earth.* Scholastic Inc., 1990.

Farndon, John. *How The Earth Works*. Reader's Digest Association, 1991.

Frank, Majorie. *202 Science Investigations.* Incentive Publications, 1990.

Giant Book of Questions and Answers. Octopus Publishing, 1990.

Herbert, Don. *Mr. Wizard's Supermarket Science.* Random House, 1980.

KIDS Discover. *Rain Forests*. KIDS Discover, 1993.

Melton, Lisa and Ladizinsky, Eric. *50 Nifty Science Experiments.* Lowell House, 1992.

Meyer, Jerome S. *Boiling Water in a Paper Cup.* Scholastic, Inc, 1970.

Morris, Dean. *Endangered Animals.* Raintree Steck-V, 1990.

National Wildlife Federation Staff. *Endangered Species.* National Wildlife, 1991.

Ontario Science Centre. *Scienceworks.* Addison-Wesley Publishing Co., 1986.

Parks, Mary. *"Making an African Rainstick." Instructor Magazine.* Jan/Feb., 1995.

Reader's Digest. *ABC'S of Nature.* Reader's Digest Association, 1984.

Russell, W. M. S. *Man, Nature, and History.* Natural History Press, 1969.

Schwartz, Linda. *Earth Book for Kids*. The Learning Works, 1990.

Stone, Lynn. *Endangered Animals.* Childrens, 1984.

Stein, Sara. *The Science Book.* Workman Publications, 1980.

Bibliography (cont.)

Toleman, Marvin. *Earth Science Activities for Grades 2–8.* Parker Publishing, 1986.

Tropical Rain Forests of the World. The Book People, 1990.

Uchitel, Sandra & Serge Michaels. *Endangered Animals of the Rain Forest.* Price Stern, 1992.

Van Cleave, Janice. *Earth Science for Every Kid.* John Wiley and Sons, 1991.

Van Cleave, Janice. *200 Gooey, Slimy, Weird and Fun Experiments.* John Wiley and Sons, 1993.

Wapole, Brenda. *175 Science Experiments to Amuse and Amaze Your Friends.* Random House, 1988.

Spanish Titles

Bornemann, E. *¡Nada de tucanes! (No Toucans Allowed!).* Lectorum, 1987.

Cowcher, Helen. *La Tigresa (Tigress).* Farrar, Strauss, & Giroux, 1993.

Suess. *El Lorax (The Lorax).* Lectorum, 1993.

Wright, Alexandra. *¿Les Echaremo de Menos? Especies en peligro de extincion (Will We Miss Them? Species in Danger of Extention).* Charlesbridge Publishing, 1993.

Technology

Cornet. *Animals of the World Series: Animals of a Living Reef, Animals of North America, and Animals of South America.* Available from Cornet/MTI Film & Video, (800)777-8100. video

Inview. *A Field Trip to the Rainforest.* Available from Sunburst, (800)321-7511. software

National Geographic Series. *STV: Rain Forest.* Available from VideoDiscovery, (800)548-3472. videodisc

Orange Cherry. *Talking Jungle Safari.* Available from CDL Software Shop, (800)637-0047. software

Partridge Film & Video. *Monkey Rain Forest.* Available from Cornet/MTI Film & Video, (800)777-8100. videodisc